Fishing Grounds Of The Gulf Of Maine

By

Walter H. Rich

Double 9
BOOKS

Fishing Grounds Of The Gulf Of Maine
by Walter H. Rich

Copyright © 2024

All Rights reserved.

No part of this publication may be reproduced, stored in a retrieval system, or transmitted in any form or by any means, electronic, mechanical, photocopying or Otherwise, without the written permission of the publisher.
The author/editor asserts the moral right to be identified as the author/editor of this work.

ISBN: 978-93-61427-42-8

Published by

DOUBLE 9 BOOKS

2/13-B, Ansari Road
Daryaganj, New Delhi – 110002
info@double9books.com
www.double9books.com
Tel. 011-40042856

This book is under public domain

ABOUT THE AUTHOR

Walter H. Rich is renowned for his knowledge in marine biology and his profound information of the aquatic ecosystems of the Gulf of Maine. His seminal paintings, "Fishing Grounds of the Gulf of Maine," stands as a testament to his meticulous research and deep ardour for the ocean. In this comprehensive manual, Rich offers precious insights into the numerous array of fish species, shellfish, and different marine existence that inhabit the rich waters of the Gulf. Drawing upon decades of firsthand revel in and clinical observation, he offers unique descriptions of the location's fishing grounds, which include their geographical capabilities, seasonal versions, and the fine strategies for catching various species. More than simply a sensible manual for anglers and fishermen, "Fishing Grounds of the Gulf of Maine" also serves as a testomony to the importance of conservation and sustainable control practices. Rich emphasizes the want for responsible stewardship of the marine surroundings to make sure the lengthy-term health and viability of the region's fisheries. With its wealth of records and Rich's attractive writing style, "Fishing Grounds of the Gulf of Maine" has become an essential aid for everybody with an interest inside the marine existence of this ecologically substantial place.

CONTENTS

PREFACE TO THE 1994 EDITION

Fishing Grounds of the Gulf of Maine by Walter H. Rich first appeared in the U.S. Department of Commerce, Bureau of Fisheries, Report of the United States Commissioner of Fisheries, for the fiscal year 1929.

When Captain Robert McLellan of Boothbay Harbor died in 1981, the employees of the Maine Department of Marine Resources contributed money to be used to purchase books in his memory, for the Department's Fishermen's Library. Captain McLellan's family was asked what purchases they would recommend, and a top priority was to somehow reprint this work on the fishing grounds. This was a book that had been helpful to Captain McLellan in his career, and one which his son, Captain Richard McLellan, found still valid and useful.

Contributions from the employees of the Department of Marine Resources paid to get this project started; film to reproduce the pages of the original text was donated by the Bigelow Laboratory for Ocean Sciences; printing costs were paid by the Department.

It is the hope of the Department and its employees that the fishermen of today will benefit from the detailed information in this publication, and that they will remember Captain Robert McLellan, a man who knew how to use books to enhance his career as a fisherman, who knew how to share his knowledge with the scientific community, and who was widely respected by fishermen and scientists alike.

INTRODUCTION

Paralleling the northeastern coast line of North America lies a long chain of fishing banks—a series of plateaus and ridges rising from the ocean bed to make comparatively shallow soundings. From very early times these grounds have been known to and visited by the adventurers of the nations of western Europe—Northman, Breton, Basque, Portuguese, Spaniard, Frenchman, and Englishman. For centuries these fishing areas have played a large part in feeding the nations bordering upon the Western Ocean, and the development of their resources has been a great factor in the exploration of the New World.

According to statistics collected by the Bureau of Fisheries, [2] these banks annually produce over 400,000,000 pounds of fishery products, which are landed in the United States; and, according to O. E. Sette, [3] annually about 1,000,000,000 pounds of cod are taken on these banks and landed in the United States, Canada, Newfoundland, France, and Portugal.

Apparently the earliest known and certainly the most extensive of these is the Great Bank of Newfoundland, so named from time immemorial. From the Flemish Cap, in 44° 06′ west longitude and 47° north latitude, marking the easternmost point of this great area, extends the Grand Bank westward and southwestward over about 600 miles of length. Thence, other grounds continue the chain, passing along through the Green Bank, St. Peters Bank, Western Bank (made up of several more or less connected grounds, such as Misaine Bank, Banquereau, The Gully, and Sable Island Bank); thence southwest through Emerald Bank, Sambro, Roseway, La Have, Seal Island Ground, Browns Bank, and Georges Bank with its southwestern extension of Nantucket Shoals.

To all these is added the long shelving area extending from the coast out to the edge of the continental plateau and stretching from the South Shoal off Nantucket to New York, making in all, from the eastern part of the Grand Bank to New York Bay, a distance of about 2,000 miles, an almost continuous extent of most productive fishing ground.

Within the bowl that is the Gulf of Maine, the outer margin of which is made by the shoaling of the water over the Seal Island Grounds, Browns Bank, and Georges Bank, this chain is further extended by another series of smaller grounds, as Grand Manan Bank, the German Bank, Jeffreys Bank,

Cashes Bank, Platts Bank, Jeffreys Ledge, Fippenies Bank, Stellwagen or Middle Bank; and again, lying inside these, this fishing area is increased by a very large number of smaller grounds and fishing spots located within a very short distance of the mainland.

All these banks are breeding places of the most valued of our food fishes—the cod, haddock, cusk, hake, pollock, and halibut—and each in its proper season furnishes fishing ground where are taken many other important species of migratory and pelagic food fishes as well as those named here. It is probable that no other fishing area equaling this in size or in productivity exists anywhere else in the world, and the figures of the total catch taken from it must show an enormous poundage and a most imposing sum representing the value of its fishery.

With the most distant of these grounds we shall not deal here, leaving them for later consideration when noting certain of the fishery operations most characteristic of them. Thus, we may treat of those well-defined areas that lie within or are adjacent to the Gulf of Maine, such as the Bay of Fundy, the Inner Grounds (those close to the mainland), the Outer Grounds (those within the gulf), the Georges area, Seal Island Grounds, and Browns Bank, these forming the outer margin of the gulf; and also make mention of certain others of those nearer offshore banks that are most closely connected with the market fishery of the three principal fishing ports within the Gulf of Maine.

ACKNOWLEDGEMENTS

As to the charts, it has been the writer's endeavor, by consulting a large number of fishing captains of long experience upon these grounds, to reduce the margin of inaccuracy as much as possible. In case of conflict of their opinion, the greatest agreement as to the facts has been accepted.

The grounds as drawn are not meant to include any definite depth curve but are meant to show certain fishing areas. It is known of course, that most species frequent the shallows and the deep water at the various seasons: also, that certain other species are found on the deeper soundings during virtually all the year. Thus, if a given area appears as a larger ground than is shown upon other charts made for navigating purposes, often this is because we have included in it a cusk ground or a hake bottom lying adjacent to the shoal as charted.

A large number of these grounds have been described before by G. Browne Goode and others, and where possible their work has been used as a basis for the present paper, with any further information or the noting of any changed condition of the grounds or difference in fishing methods employed upon them that was obtainable.

Grateful acknowledgment is hereby made to the many captains who furnished information that, made the drawing of the charts possible and for the facts used in the descriptions of the fishing grounds.

With the offshore banks, particularly with the Georges area and Browns Bank and to a certain extent, also, the western portion of the Inner Grounds, the writer has had a considerable personal acquaintance from which to draw.

For the geographical and historical data the writer has quoted freely from various modern authors, who, in their turn, have drawn their facts from older records. Among those quoted are Holmes's American Annals; Parkman's Pioneers of France in the New World; Southgates History of Scarburo; Abbott and Elwell's History of Maine; Willis's History of Maine; Sabine's Report on the Principal Fisheries of the American Seas; A History of the Discovery of the East Coast of North America, by Dr. John G. Kohl, of Bremen, Germany; various chapters of Hakluyt's Voyages; the Journal of John Jocelyn, Gent.; and New England Trials of the famous Captain John Smith.

GULF OF MAINE

Geographical & Historical Name

What is apparently the earliest mention of this body of water appears on some old Icelandic charts that show, roughly, Cape Cod Bay in their southern areas and the Bay of Fundy in the northern. On these maps the cape itself was shown on the "Promontory of Vinland" and was given the name Kialarnes, or the Ship's Nose, from its resemblance in form to the high upturned prow of the old Norse ships. To the entire area of the gulf was given the title Vinland's Haf.

Oviedo (Historia General de las Indias) sometimes names this gulf the Arcipelago de La Tramontana, or the Arcipelago Septentrional—the northern archipelago. He gives us to understand that he, himself, or Chaves, had this information from the Report and Survey of Gomez, who, in his search for a northwest passage to Asia in 1525, "discovered all these coasts lying between 41° and 41° 30' north". As a matter of fact, his careful explorations certainly covered all the territory between 40 and 45 degrees.

The Spanish navigators who followed Gomez, in describing these coasts, when indicating this gulf, usually named it in honor of Gomez, the first of their nation to make a careful survey of its shores. Thus it became known as the Arcipelago de Estevan Gomez, and the mainland behind it as La Tierra de Gomez. It was so named on the map of Ribero in 1529 who thus acknowledged the source of his information.

The Biscayans followed Gomez but later gave way to the French fishermen, who followed down the chain of banks extending southward from the Grand Bank and entered these waters by way of Cape Sable. These gave to it the name Gulf of Norumbega or Sea of Norumbega. The name Norumbega was for a time applied to the coast lands and to the inland country stretching away indefinitely westward and northwestward from the waters of the gulf.

Later, with the coming of the English and the establishment of their colony in Massachusetts, the title Massachusetts Bay came into general use, although this name was afterwards restricted to the smaller section of the gulf at present so termed.

The charter of Gorges (in April, 1639) designated the territory deeded to him as the Province or County of Maine, [4] whence, perhaps, the modern custom of referring to these waters as the Gulf of Maine may have arisen. This latest name seems especially appropriate, in view of the fact that the present State of Maine lying directly opposite its entrance capes, stretches along the inner borders of the gulf and with its deeply indented shore line occupies by far the greatest section of its coasts. Thus the title has finally come into general use and acceptance in modern times. Apparently it was first officially proposed and used by the Edinburgh Encyclopedia in 1832 [5] and later was adopted by the United States Coast Survey.

Description

A very striking and peculiar body of water is this Gulf of Maine, markedly different in character from any other of the bays on the coast line of the eastern United States. Especially does it differ in the depth of its coastal waters, where in all the others, except the much smaller New York Bay, the shoal water is found extending far out from the land.

In the Gulf of Maine, however, with the single exception of the vicinity of Ammens Rock on the eastern part of Cashes Bank, the entire central area presents navigable deep water having a mean depth of 100 fathoms, out of which rise the various underwater plateaus, whose depths average about 50 fathoms and which constitute the larger of the fishing grounds. In addition to these, many smaller banks and "fishing spots" are found nearer the land where they lie a along the 50-fathom curve.

In general this curve lies at a distance of about 16 miles from the coast line, but in many instances it approaches much neared to the mainland. From this 50-fathom depth the soundings decrease very gradually to the 20 and 10 fathom marks.

These latter soundings are often held far in toward the coast line, even carrying the deep water well into the river mouths, so that in deeply indented hays, in long inlets running far into land, in the river mouths, the deep water behind the rocky headlands, or in the lee of the thousands of surf-washed islands that line the coast, are found innumerable safe anchorages within easy run of the fishing grounds, where the fleets may take shelter from a sudden blow or await the arrival of a "fish day," when conditions may permit "making a set" under the hardships of winter fishing.

If the marine features of this region are radically different from those of other coastal bodies of the eastern United States, so, too, the shore land, battered as it has been by sea and storm or worn by glacial action or Arctic currents, is no less remarkable.

No other section of the eastern United States has a similar coast, so serrated, indented, and rugged, as has this shore line of the Gulf of Maine. Here the battering by the forces of nature has resulted in making thousands of safe harbors and havens for the navigator. All along shore are strewn hundreds of islands, a characteristic feature of the region and one noted with wonder by every early explorer. [6] These islands, if near the land, are beautiful and smiling; if in the open sea, of rugged grandeur; and mainland and island alike are inhabited by a numerous and hardy race of fisher folk.

The tides within the Gulf of Maine have a very great rise and fall as compared with other waters in this region. At the south of Cape Cod tides are seldom over 4 feet in their range, but beginning at once at the north of Cape Cod with a rise of from 7 to 10 feet these increase quite constantly as they go eastward reaching about 28 feet in the neighborhood of Passamaquoddy Bay, to touch their highest point in the Bay of Fundy, where in many places is a rise and fall of 50 feet, and in some few places tides of 70 feet are reported. These Fundy tides probably are the greatest in the world.

This great ebb and flow of water serves to aid shipbuilding and the launching of vessels as well as to carry the deep water far up into the inlets of the coast and into the mouths of the rivers, making these navigable for crafts of considerable size well into the land or up to the lowest falls of the streams.

The climate here is one of extremes, and, lying as it does between 42° and 45° north latitude, the region may be said to be cold. Apparently the waters of the Gulf of Maine are not affected by any stray current from the Gulf Stream, which passes at a considerable distance from its mouth, thus doing little to temper the cold of this area either on land or at sea. Whether these waters are cooled further by any flow from the Labrador Current may be questioned.

The winters are long, usually bringing heavy snowfalls; and strong gales are frequent during much of the fall and winter season. Perhaps the most dangerous of these "blows" come out of the mountain to the north and northwest of the gulf. Thus, in addition to the uncertainty of an opportunity to set gear when once upon the fishing grounds, the winter fishing here is not without its element of serious danger. While the ice crop in northern New England never fails, yet, perhaps because of the strong tidal currents of these waters, the principal harbors rarely are closed by ice, or, if closed, for but a few days only.

While the summers are fairly mild and in certain parts of them even extremely hot, fogs are heavy and virtually continuous during the "dog days" (July 20 to September 1). when southerly and south-westerly breezes bring the warm moist air from the Gulf Stream into the cooler currents from the land. The fogs of Fundy are especially noted, even in these waters. During the summer seasons winds from the east and north bring the only clear weather experienced in the outer chain of fishing grounds.

The main body of the gulf lies approximately between 42° and 45° north latitude. It is in form like a deep bowl whose outer rim is made by Georges Bank and Browns Bank, with a narrow, deep-water spillway between: its area is half encircled in the arms of the mainland, two conspicuous headlands reaching bodily seaward to mark its wide entrance at the opposite sides—Cape Cod, Mass. [7] on the western side, and Cape Sable, [8] Nova Scotia, on the eastern flank, distant from each other about 230 miles. These two capes range with each other about ENE. and WSW, thus matching alike the general trend of the coast line, of the island chains and of the offshore ledges within this area.

From a base line connecting these outposts of the gulf the distance to the Maine coast opposite averages about 120 miles. From Cape Sable, at its eastern end, the coast trends for some distance to the northwest, whence a continuation of this course strikes the coast of Maine near West Quoddy Head at a distance of rather more than 110 miles. From West Quoddy head to Cape Elizabeth (in a direct line about 160 miles) the coast, in general rough, rocky, and with many lofty headlands is extremely irregular and deeply indented and follows a general course of WSW. Thence, the coast, lower and becoming more and more sandy, begins to trend more decidedly south-west until it reaches Boston, when it turns to the southeast, and to the east toward Cape Cod.

But this is not the entire story. There remain outside of these stated limits the Bay of Fundy in the north, with a possible area of 3,000 square miles; and at the south Cape Cod Bay, whose area, with that of the waters west of a perpendicular drawn from the western end of the base line that strikes the land in the vicinity of Portsmouth, N. H. makes an additional section containing close to 1,500 square miles. Within the limits thus inclosed there are, roughly, 30,000 square miles of most productive ground most intensively fished through all the year.

The Bay of Fundy is divided at its head by Cape Chignecto, making two branches to north and to east—Chignecto Bay and Minas Basin. With these smaller areas, lying as they do entirely within the territorial limits of Canada, American fishermen have little to do, although both are valuable and productive fishing grounds.

BAY OF FUNDY

At the different seasons of the year the entire Bay of Fundy [9] is a fishing ground for sardines and large herring; and while these are of somewhat less importance in recent years than formerly, the principal fisheries of this region still center around the herring industries—the supplying of the canning factories with the small herring used as sardines and the taking of large herring for food and bait. The sardine industry of the State of Maine is largely concentrated in the district about and including Eastport and Lubec, where about 30 of the 59 factories and 16 of the 43 operating firms are located; so that, while the herring catches of recent years have fallen much short of their former proportions, they still show imposing figures.

In the past much of the catch was taken in St. Andrews (Passamaquoddy) Bay and along the north shore of the Bay of Fundy to Lepreau Bay and Point. Lepreau. Of late years virtually no herring have been taken in these waters, in which the herring schools that arrive in October were accustomed to remain until spring. Of past fishing in this locality Capt. Sumner Stuart, of Lubec, says:

"The herring left St. Andrews Bay and the North Shore about 1885. There is no summer netting there now. Those waters and Lepreau Bay were formerly very productive fishing grounds, it being not unusual to take 5,000 (count) big herrings (food fish) in a single haul. These were mainly spring and winter fishing grounds for large herring. The fish seem to have disappeared from all these grounds at about the same time. [10]

"In past years (25 to 30 years ago) small herring were driven ashore in such quantities by their enemies—squid, silver hake and dogfish— that it sometimes became necessary for the authorities at St. John to use a snowplow to cover them where they lay decaying on the beach."

From the statistics of the sardine and smoked-herring industry for the year 1924 (a year, be it noted, in which the sardine industry almost reached low—level mark for the pack) the waters of the Bay of Fundy furnished to American purchasers alone a total of herring for smoking and canning purposes amounting to 76,756,250 pounds valued to the fishermen at $957,665. This showing, poor as it is when compared with the figures of other years, by no means represents the herring fishery as an unimportant industry. There still remains to be accounted for the catch of herring of Grand Manan and the neighboring Canadian Provinces.

A new source of profit to the fishermen in this industry has been developed in the purchase of herring scales by firms engaged in the manufacture of artificial pearls. For this purpose there were collected at Eastport and Lubec 700,000 pounds of herring scales, valued at $39,000; and a further amount was taken at Grand Manan of 140,000 pounds, valued at $7,000. With other entrants already in the field, this branch of the industry bids fair to grow to still greater importance.

An estimate of the number of weirs in St. Andrews Bay, by Capt. Guilford Mitchell of Eastport, Me., is as follows: Canadian: 1921: 126 weirs 1923: 40 weirs Calais to Eastport: 1921: 35 weirs; 1923: 7 weirs Total number in operation, 1923, Canadian, about 300; American less than 130.

North Shore and coast of Nova Scotia. Along the North Shore and from Yarmouth to Cape Sable, over a hard bottom, cod abound. The western shore of Nova Scotia is virtually all fishing ground for cod, haddock, hake, and cusk, but trawling is somewhat handicapped here by strong tides and rocky bottom, these combining to destroy much gear. Halibut are somewhat unusual on this western shore except about the mouth of the Bay of Fundy, but in summer these fish are occasionally found close inshore along the southwest coast, going somewhat beyond Digby to the northward. Haddocking is quite an important industry off Yarmouth, Nova Scotia, during the winter, the sets being of rather short duration and made at the slack of the tide at high water. This practice is made necessary by the heavy tidal currents on these grounds.

The whole western coast of Nova Scotia is herring ground at some season of the year. "Drifting" for herring was formerly a considerable industry from Digby to Briers Island, but in these last few years it has not been important, although the year 1927 had a very good run of large food fish. This western coast is also an important fishing area for lobster men.

Swordfishing in the Bay of Fundy was formerly profitable in September, although these fish were never so numerous here as upon the outer shore of Nova Scotia.

St. Marys Bay is a summer herring ground. Good haddocking may be had here, also, from April 15 to October 15, with the period from the opening of the fishing in April up to July 15 the best of it.

The mackerel fishery of the Bay of Fundy seems of comparatively small importance in these latter years. The local fishermen say that the fish can not stem the tides of these waters! The abundance of small herring should be an inducement sufficient to bring them here. Apparently these fish pass straight inshore northwesterly and reach the coast of Maine. A considerable amount of this species is taken by traps and by netting in St. Marys Bay and in the general vicinity of Yarmouth, Nova Scotia, as at Cranberry Head, Burns Point. Beaver River, Woods Harbor, and at various other points between Yarmouth and Cape Sable; but the inner waters of the Bay of Fundy show very slim catches when compared with the great amount taken on the outer shores of Nova Scotia in a normal mackerel season. It has been 32 years, it is said, since any number of mackerel have been "hooked" in St. Mary's Bay.

Lurcher Shoal. This lies WSW, from Cape St, Mary 19 miles and WNW, from Cape Fourchu, distant 13 miles, it is an irregularly shaped piece of bottom, a rocky ground, about 5 miles long, north and south, by 3 miles wide, There are a number of "nubbles" arising to 5, 7, and 9 fathom depths— with a spot reported as having only 12 feet of water over it—rising from the average depths over the rest of the shoal of from 13 to 15 fathoms. Over this generally rocky bottom are scattered patches of gravel and of shells, Depths about the shoal are from 30 to 50 fathoms over a bottom consisting mostly of stones, Tide rips are very heavy here, The seasons and species found here are as on Trinity: cod, haddock, pollock, and herring, it is a good lobster ground.

Trinity Shoal. This shoal, 14 miles N. by W. from Cape Fourchu and 7½ miles SW. from Cape St Mary, with a rocky bottom upon it and over an indefinite area about it, is perhaps 3 miles long, NE and SW, by some 2 miles wide. Near the center is a rock, uncovered at low water, but over the greater part of the shoal there are depths of from 6 to 10 fathoms, with an average of from 12 to 16 fathoms over the sandy and stony ground about it. There is a strong tide rip here on the eastern and northeastern part known as Flood Tide Eddy, where is good fishing by hand line for pollock in September and October. Cod and haddock are taken here in small amounts by trawling. It is a herring ground also, and there is a lobster ground on the shoal and all about it.

A cod ground extends offshore SW from Briers Island, beginning about 5 miles out from the island and extending to about 18 miles from the land. Its width is about 4 miles. Depths over this area are from 40 to 60 fathoms over a hard, shelly bottom. Cod are taken here in from 30 to 44 fathoms on the shoal ground running from 5 miles from Gull Rock and the South-West Ledges down to the Lurcher Shoal, a distance of about 22 miles. Between these points fishing is done mostly by hand-lining "at a drift." Cod are taken over the ledges in 5 fathoms of water and thence out to 60 fathoms about them from August to November. Pollock are taken by the same method.

The best season is August. September, and October. This is a good lobster ground.

Northwest Ledge. Lies about 3 3/4 miles northwesterly from Briers Island. This is a piece of rocky bottom about 2 miles long by something less than 1 mile wide with depths of from 2 to 10 fathoms over the ledge and soundings of 12 to 30 fathoms on the gravelly ground about it. Cod are found here in good number from September to November, inclusive, and are taken by hand-lining. Pollock also are taken here in summer, "drailing" by hand line.

A narrow piece of rocky ground with somewhat greater depths connects this with Batsons Shoal, some 5 miles SW., the two thus making what is virtually one piece of ground. Depths on Batsons Shoal are rather less than on Northwest Ledge, but the methods of fishing, the species taken, and the seasons of their abundance are the same on both. The bottom all about these two grounds is rocky, with from 20 to 40 fathoms inside of them, but this deepens rapidly to 100 fathoms over rocks and coarse gravel outside of them to W. and NW.

West-Northwest Rips and the Flat Ground. These lie WNW from Briers Island, extending offshore about 18 miles. On the eastern end of this area, two parallel shoals, about 1½ miles across and having 50-fathom depths between them, rise from the 100-fathom depths of water over the muddy ground around them to reach 15 fathoms on the landward end of the rips, deepening to 35 fathoms off the western part, where the two ridges come together at about 9 miles distance from Briers Island, to carry on to the westward over the Flat Ground, which extends to a distance of about 18 miles from the island.

This Flat Ground, deepening gradually westward, averages to have 50 fathoms of water over a level, gravelly, and rocky bottom, to pitch down suddenly, as do all other slopes of this piece of ground, to the 100-fathom depth, which prevails on all sides of The Rips. Currents are very strong here, as elsewhere in these waters, so that trawls are set only on the slack of the tides, beginning about one hour before and remaining down until about one hour after these periods. Formerly this was a good ground for the taking of large herring. In these days The Rips furnish good cod and haddock fishing for the entire year, with hake abundant at all times on the mud about them. In fact; virtually all the ground from this point south to the Lurcher Shoal furnishes good fishing for these species.

Boars Head Ground (also called Inner Ground). This parallels the coast about 4 miles N. by NW from the Head, at Petit Passage, into St. Marys Bay. This ground is about 4 miles long by 3 miles wide, having depths from 55 to

65 fathoms over a hard bottom of broken ground. Cod are most numerous here from April to July, inclusive; haddock from July to September, inclusive. Hake are found here in summer and early fall, principally on the muddy ground between this and the next fishing ground—the Outer Ground.

Outer Ground. This is about 3 miles long by 2 miles wide, lies about 9 miles out from the main on the same bearing as the Inner Ground, and is visited by the same species, their periods of abundance upon this piece of bottom being the same as on the former ground. Virtually all taking of ground fish on these grounds is done by hand-lining, though the practice of trawl fishing has come more and more into use in recent years.

Head and Horns. A shoal of 68 fathoms, about 2 miles long in a NNE and SSW direction by 1 mile wide, lies due north from the Boars Head of Long Island. Here is a hard bottom where good cod fishing is had during the spring and summer. Hand-lining from the bottom is carried on in summer for pollock. Haddock are few here, these appearing mostly in the summer. Depths about the ground average 80 fathoms over mud and stones.

Sandy Cove Ground. Lies offshore NNE about 7 miles from West Sandy Cove. It has from 40 to 50 fathoms of water over a sandy bottom, lying parallel with the coast, about 4 miles long by 2 miles wide. Cod are abundant on this ground from May to July, hake coming somewhat later. As were most of the grounds of this vicinity, this ground was mainly a hand-line spot, but in recent years fishing here has been done mostly by the trawl method.

Inner Sandy Cove Grounds. About 2 miles NNW. from West Sandy Cove. These are 3 miles long NNE. and SSW. by ½ mile wide. Both hand-lining and trawling methods of fishing are in use here, but the trawl is fast displacing the older gear. Depths are about 35 fathoms over a sandy bottom and 50 fathoms all about it. Species and their seasons of abundance are as on the Outer Sandy Cove Ground. Almost anywhere between Spencer Island and Cape Split there is good haddock fishing in June and July and cod fishing in May and June. Depths are from 16 to 40 fathoms: the bottom is generally stony, with considerable areas of gravel. The fishing is done principally by trawling, rather short "sets" being made. Off Cape Split are considerable whirlpools, which, with spring tides, are very dangerous. These sometimes run 9 knots an hour.

Spencer Island. Almost anywhere between Spencer Island and Cape Split there is good haddock fishing in June and July and cod fishing in May and June. Depths are from 16 to 40 fathoms: the bottom is generally stony, with considerable areas of gravel. The fishing is done principally by trawling, rather short "sets" being made. Off Cape Split are considerable whirlpools, which, with spring tides, are very dangerous. These sometimes run 9 knots an hour.

Isle au Haute. Lies far up within the bay 9 miles W. ½ S. from Cape Chignecto. All about this island are good summer haddock grounds with fair cod fishing. The latter are taken by trawling principally. Depths about the island are from 9 to 14 fathoms, deepening offshore to 35, the average depths being 22 to 27 fathoms. North of the island the bottom is generally sandy; elsewhere much of the ground is rocky or stony, with here and there a small patch of gravelly ground. To the S. of this ground, toward the Nova Scotia shore and to within 2 miles of the coast, the bottom is mainly muddy and of little account as a fishing ground. Tides are very heavy on all the inner grounds of the Bay of Fundy.

Quaco Ledges. This ground lies about 10 miles SE, from Quaco Head and is out at low tide, the water about the ledges having depths from 14 to 30 fathoms over a bottom of stones and gravel, There is a heavy tide rip over these ledges when covered, These furnish good pollock fishing in the summer months, and cod fishing is carried on here by hand-lining from May to July.

Salmon Netting Ground. A salmon-netting ground lies off about the Mouth Harbour and St, John Harbour, where these fish are netted, for the most part during June and July, when they are en route to the St, John River, where are their spawning grounds.

Ingalls Shoal. This is the name given by some of the fishermen of the vicinity to a shoal lying about midway between Digby, Nova Scotia, and Point Lepreau, New Brunswick. This ground is about 9 miles long. NE. and SW., by about 5 miles wide. It lies about 22 miles NW. from Digby and 18 or 20 miles from Point Lepreau. The depths are from 35 fathoms on the shoalest area (where is a piece of ground some 4 miles long by 1 mile wide near the center of the bank, lying in a NE. and SW. direction), the bottom sloping away from this on all sides to 47 or even 55 fathoms in a few places. The bottom is mostly of sand and gravel or of small stones over much of the ground except for the shoal parts, where it is mainly rocky. This piece of fishing ground furnishes good cod fishing in June, July, and August, which formerly was carried on by hand-lining but now, as elsewhere in the bay, is more and more becoming a trawl fishery. Haddock and pollock also are taken here in fair amounts.

Mussel Shoal Ground. This is a mussel-covered bottom lying 8 miles ESE. from the Eastern Wolf and 9 miles from Point Lepreau. It runs in an E. and W. direction and is about 2 miles long by 1 mile wide. Depths are from 40 to 50 fathoms. This is a mussel and scallop bed, where large cod are usually in abundance in winter. Pollock are plenty here in June, and hake are here and in the surrounding Hake Ground in all the summer months.

The Wolves. These make a group of small islands lying N. ½ E. from Grand Manan, distant 8 or 10 miles. On the bottom of rocks and gravel, extending about a mile from the shores of these, in depths of from 18 to 34 fathoms, small boats and small vessels take a quantity of fish by trawl and hand line. These are mainly haddock and cod grounds in May and June and pollock grounds in June and July. It is also a winter lobster ground for Canadian fishermen.

The Wolves Bank. This bank lies between The Wolves and Grand Manan, distant about 8 miles from East Quoddy Light, SE. ½ E. Marks: The Coxcomb showing to the eastward and just touching on the western edge of Green Island: bring the heads of Grand Manan to form The Armchair, and White Horse and Simpson Island into range. This is a small-boat ground of scarcely more than 6 acres, with depths of 18 to 30 fathoms on a bottom of rocks and mud. Species and seasons are as on The Wolves. Southeast from The Wolves from 2 to 20 miles lies a piece of muddy bottom where hake are usually abundant in summer.

Campobello and vicinity. Fair quantities of haddock and cod are found between Grand Manan and the American shore in the North Channel (Grand Manan Channel) between West Quoddy Head and Grand Manan in depths of from 40 to 50 fathoms, over a bottom of rocks, mud, and sand in June, July, and August and up to September 15, while hake is the most abundant species present.

No haddock or cod are on these grounds in winter. Halibut are taken in similar numbers in the North Channel in May, June, and July. Pollock are taken on the western side of Campobello Island, near the eastern side of Indian Island, and at the mouth of the channel between Campobello and Casco Bay Island. In all these places are strong tidal eddies. Some fish are taken by seining, but most are caught by hook and line in a small-boat fishery lasting from June 1 to September 1.

All around Campobello and Deer Island and on the New Brunswick shore as far as St. John are located weirs, which furnish large quantities of herring to the factories at Eastport and Lubec.

Passamaquoddy Bay. [11] Depths here are from 10 to 24 fathoms, even 30 fathoms where the St. Croix River passes out into the sea. In general the bottom is muddy, although there are rocky patches. In most years a school of cod "strikes" here in April, the early corners being mostly of small size, but the later arrivals may reach 30, 40, or even 60 pounds. Haddock sometimes make their appearance in the bay as early as May 1, remaining through August. Hake, also, are present from June to September, but this excellent fish is held of little account by local fishermen. A considerable flounder industry is developing in these waters, the fish being taken in specially devised traps as well as by the smaller otter trawls.

Passamaquoddy Bay is also a spring netting ground for herring (food fish), and there are also many weirs in operation here each year whose catch goes to the factories of Eastport and Lubec for canning as sardines. Pollock are very abundant, and a great deal of fishing for them is carried on from June to October, both by seine and hand line. At times the pollock completely fill the many herring weirs, until, from their numbers, there is no market for them. Pollock are also abundant at the same season and are taken by the same methods in the St. Croix River, though perhaps they leave the river a month earlier in the fall.

The Mud Hake Grounds. These grounds extend about N. and S. between Campobello and The Wolves and from about West Quoddy Head to Grand Manan. Their length is about 15 to 18 miles and their width 3½ miles. This is a summer ground much used by Canadian fishermen out of Campobello, Grand Manan, and Beaver Harbor. It is said to be the best hake grounds in this vicinity. Depths are from 45 to 60 fathoms, and fishing is done by trawls and hand lines.

There is a stretch of muddy bottom from Point Lepreau and Beaver Harbor to Grand Manan, which furnishes good hake fishing. In general, the bottom on the western side of the Bay of Fundy is muddy. Off Beaver Harbor on a mud bottom with 30 fathoms of water cod are found the year around, although this fishery is mainly carried on in the winter in small craft from Beaver Harbor and Campobello, mostly by trawling, but some hand-lining is carried on.

Beaver Harbor. There is a stretch of muddy bottom from Point Lepreau and Beaver Harbor to Grand Manan, which furnishes good hake fishing. In general, the bottom on the western side of the Bay of Fundy is muddy. Off Beaver Harbor on a mud bottom with 30 fathoms of water cod are found the year around, although this fishery is mainly carried on in the winter in small craft from Beaver Harbor and Campobello, mostly by trawling, but some hand-lining is carried on.

Grand Manan Bank. This bank is at the entrance of the Bay of Fundy, SW. ½ S. from the southwest head of Grand Manan Island from which the northern part of the bank is 15 miles distant. From Mount Desert Rock, E. by S., it is 45 miles distant. The bank is 10 miles long and 5 miles wide, extending in a NE. and SW. direction. The bottom is mostly stones and gravel, the depths running from 24 to 45 fathoms. Soundings of 18 and 21 fathoms are found on the northeast part.

Cod (especially abundant when the June school is on the ground) and pollock are the principal fish. Haddock are not usually abundant, although sometimes they are plentiful in the fall from late September to December; hake are fairly abundant on the mud between Grand Manan Bank and the Middle Ground (in The Gully). This is a good halibut bank, the fish being in 33 to 60 fathoms in June and July; the southwest soundings and the southeast soundings are most productive always.

The best fishing season is from April to October, when the fish come to this bank to feed. In the spring the fish, other than halibut, are mostly on the southwest part, but later (July to October) the best fishing is had on the northern edge of the ground. The very best herring fishing for large herring (food fish) occurs on this bank in June and July. In general, this is a small-vessel ground fished by craft from Cutler, Eastport, Grand Manan, and, to a less extent, Yarmouth, Nova Scotia, with an occasional visit by craft from Portland and Rockland, chiefly trawlers of moderate size.

Tides run NE. in flood and SW. on the ebb and are quite strong, the flood being the heaviest. Because of these powerful currents, fishing is somewhat difficult, it being necessary to make sets at the slack of the tides, getting the gear over and traveling with the finish of the current, to take it up and come back with the tide's return.

Clarks Ground. This lies SSE. from White head 4 ½ miles (just inside the Bulkhead) and has depths from 6 to 14 fathoms over a rocky bottom. Here are very heavy rips on the ebb tide. This is a good summer ground for pollock, cod, and halibut, and it is a good herring-netting ground in the season.

Southern Head Reef. The chain of reefs extending S from White Head Island is all good ground in summer for cod and for pollock, also, when the herring schools are on this ground. Currents are very heavy here. The ledges that make up this reef are more or less connected. Among these are Brazil Shoal, Tinker, Inner Diamond, Outer Diamond, Crawleys, Rans, Proprietor (Foul Ground), and the Old Proprietor. While virtually all this reef is pollock ground, Crawleys and Rans perhaps furnish the best fishing.

Gravelly. Lying about 5 or 6 miles SE. by S. from White Head, this piece of bottom has about 25-fathom depths over a rocky bottom. This is a cod and pollock ground in their season. While an occasional halibut is taken here in summer. Heavy tide rips occur here also.

The Soundings. Mentioned elsewhere as a herring ground, these lie outside the Bulkhead Rips 8 or 9 miles SE. from White Head. There are 30 or 40 fathoms of water here over a rock bottom, where pollock and cod are found in good number in July, August, and September, and a certain amount of halibut in summer.

Bulkhead Rips, also called The Ripplings. This is a long rocky barrier rising sharply from the deep water about it to depths of from 12 to 20 fathoms. Here are found cod, haddock, hake, and pollock in abundance from June 1 to October 31. Apparently all are feeding on the small herring, so numerous in this vicinity at this season. Virtually no haddock are found on the grounds in the near neighborhood of Grand Manan in winter. The Ripplings were formerly one of the principal fishing grounds of the herring netters but of late years have been less productive.

Cards Reef. The depths here are from 28 to 30 fathoms, over rocks, and the ground lies 3 miles S. by E. from the Old Proprietor and 9 miles from White Head. This is a cod and haddock ground from June to November.

Gannet Rock. This lies east of the Murre Ledges. All about it is good ground in from 40 to 70 fathoms over a hard bottom. Cod are found here in good number from March to May, and halibut are taken here from March to May, inclusive.

Southeast Ground and Gravel Bottom. These lie S. of Seal Island, forming an extensive piece of fairly level ground extensive piece of fairly level ground. The western part bears a little E. of S. and the eastern part about ESE. from the island. It is about 5 or 10 miles in diameter. While this is really but one piece of ground, the eastern part is called the Southeast Ground and the western part, from the nature of its bottom, the Gravel Bottom. The eastern portion is muddy and has 40 to 60 fathoms. The western has 35 to 40 fathoms. It is a good cod ground in winter and spring. Haddock are present from November to March, inclusive; hake in summer. Fishing is done mainly by trawling by sloops and vessels.

Machias Seal Island. Nineteen miles E. by S. from Moosabec Light. This furnishes good ground in the water all about it, where depths are from 15 to 54 fathoms over a generally rocky and uneven bottom. In summer cod, haddock, and pollock are abundant here, the cod and haddock remaining all winter. The fishery is carried on mostly by the smaller vessels from Maine ports, principally those from Cutler, with an occasional visit by larger craft, usually from the Portland fleet. This ground is not much visited in winter. Fishing is done by trawling and hand-lining.

Gannet Rock. This lies east of the Murre Ledges. All about it is good ground in from 40 to 70 fathoms over a hard bottom. Cod are found here in good number from March to May, and halibut are taken here from March to May, inclusive.

Table 1—Fishing Grounds of the Bay of Fundy Area of the Gulf of Maine, showing the principal species taken upon them.

Fishing ground	Cod	Haddock	Hake	Pollock	Cusk	Halibut	Herring	Mackerel	Lobsters	Miscellaneous
Bay of Fundy	x	x	x	x	x		[1] x		x	
North Shore and Nova Scotia	x	x	x	x	x		x		x	
Lurcher Shoal	x	x		x			x		x	
Trinity Shoal	x	x		x			x		x	
Cod Ground	x			x						
Northwest Ledges	x			x						
WNW. Rips, Flat Ground	x	x	x				x			
Inner Ground, Boars Head Ground	x	x	x							
Outer Ground	x	x	x							
Head and Horns	x			x					x	
Sandy Cove Grounds	x		x							
Inner Sandy Cove Grounds	x		x							
Spencer Island Grounds	x	x								
Isle au Haute Ground	x	x								
Quaco Ledges	x			x						
Salmon Ground										[2] x
Ingalls Shoal	x	x		x						
Mussel Shoal	x		x	x						
The Wolves	x	x		x					x	
The Wolves Bank	x	x		x						
Campobello	x	x	x	x	x		[3] x			
Passamaquoddy Bay	x	x	x	x	x		[3] x		x	[4] x
Mud Hake Ground				x						
Beaver Harbor	x									
Grand Manan	x	x	x	x	x		[1] x		x	
Peters Bank	x		x						x	
Clarks Bank	x			x	x	x				

[1] Large herring and sardine herring.   [2] Salmon.   [3] Sardine herring.   [4] Flounders.

Table 1—continued

Fishing ground	Cod	Haddock	Hake	Pollock	Cusk	Halibut	Herring	Mackerel	Lobsters	Miscellaneous
Southern Head Reef	x			x			[1] x			
Gravelly	x			x		x				
Soundings	x			x		x	[1] x			
Bulkhead, Ripplings	x	x	x	x			[1] x			
Cards Reef	x	x								
Gannet Rock	x					x				
Southeast Ground	x	x		x		x				
Southwest Ledges				x			[1] x			
Machias Seal Island	x	x		x						

[1] Large herring.

INNER GROUNDS

Under this heading are listed those grounds of the innermost chain of shoals, ledges, and "fishing spots", patches of rocky and gravelly bottom, the deeper water between them being over the muddy ground, which line the coast of the Gulf of Maine, making of it an almost continuous piece of fishing ground. In the Reports of the United States Bureau of Fisheries, on which all the statistics of the catch and value of the various species quoted in this report are based, these figures are grouped under the heading "Shore".

The larger and more important of these grounds are outcroppings along the edge of the 50-fathom curve and lie at distances varying from 12 to 20 miles offshore; but there are many inside this line, and where the deep water of the Gulf of Maine extends so far inshore some are close in to the land. Thus, nearly all are within comparatively easy reach even for the smaller craft (where these all now have power) and so furnish productive fishing for a large fleet of gill netters and sloops (small craft of from 5 to 10 tons net) and to the myriad of "under-ton" boats (of less than 5 tons net), all these being enabled to run offshore, "make a set," and return the same day.

With the uncertainties of the weather and the hazards of the winter fishing, very often the large vessels also follow this practice on those not too frequent "fish days" (when conditions permit fishing "outside ") that intervene between the storms; and with the scarcity of fish in the markets usual to the season and the consequent better price for the catch, with ordinary fishing luck they are well paid for doing so.

The fish of these shore grounds, due perhaps to the greater abundance of food here, are thought to be distinctly superior in quality to those of the same species taken on the offshore banks. The cod and the haddock, especially, of the Gulf of Maine are particularly well conditioned fish and are noted for their excellence.

The figures presented in Table 2 show only a fraction of the catch from the Inner Grounds, since they deal entirely with the fares of fishing vessels of 5 net tons and over. There are literally thousands of the so-called "licensed" or "under-tonned" boats, mainly gill-netters, that take millions of pounds from these waters annually, principally cod and haddock.

On the Maine coast and across the line in New Brunswick there are more than 300 weirs which furnished to American smokers and canners during the year 1923 (whose figures have been chosen as representing an average season) 77,000,000 pounds of herring. On the coast of Massachusetts there are 50 or more weirs and fish traps, and from the Isle of Shoals to Pemaquid Point in Maine there are more than 50 floating traps in the various bays, on the points of offshore islands, or even in the open sea, and all these take a rich harvest from these waters. Then, too, there is the lobster fishery, more important in the Gulf of Maine than anywhere else in the United States.

Of these various branches of the fisheries industries few statistics are available, yet we may say that the figures of the 1919 census showed that the "under-ton" boats mentioned landed 5,324,426 pounds of fish at the port of Boston, mostly of cod and haddock, and that the same type of craft in 1923 landed at Portland, Me., more than 3,000,000 pounds, principally of ground fish. We also know that every island, hamlet, village, town, and city along this nearly 4,000 'miles of coast line takes its toll from the sea.

Lukes Rock. This rock lies S. by E. 3 miles from Moosabec Light, circular in shape, and about 1 mile in diameter. Depths are from 25 to 35 fathoms; the bottom is rocks, gravel, and mud. This is mainly a small-boat fishing ground, but there is some vessel fishing. Hake are taken here from June to September, inclusive; cod are present about the rocks the year around. Pollock are here in spring and fall, and haddock from December to February, inclusive. Fishing is by trawl and hand line.

Newfound Ground. A small rocky spot about 1/4 mile across with an automatic buoy in the center for guidance into the Bay of Fundy. This is a small-boat ground having depths averaging 18 fathoms. It lies about 3 miles S. by W. from Moosabec Light. Species and seasons are as on Lukes Rock. Fishing is by trawl and hand line.

Henrys Rock. Five miles SW. by S. from Moosabec Light. 1/4 mile in diameter, and 30 fathoms over a level bottom. Fishing is done by hand line and trawl. Cod are present the year around, a few haddock in the fall, hake in the summer but not in the fall, and pollock in spring and fall.

Handspike Ground. Eight miles SW. by S. from Moosabec Light, nearly circular in form, and ¼ mile across. It has a bottom of rocks and depths of from 35 to 40 fathoms. Species and seasons are the same as on Lukes Rock, but mainly cod and pollock are taken here by trawl and hand line.

Western Egg Rock. This is SW. from Moosabec Light, 8 miles distant, lying in a NE. and SW. direction, 3 miles long by 1 mile wide. The bottom is irregular, sharp, and rocky and has 25 to 30 fathoms. Fishing here is mostly by hand line, the ground being said to be too rough for trawling. This is a small-boat ground, and fishing is done mainly in the summer season. Cod and pollock are taken in the spring, summer, and fall; haddock are present in spring and fall; and cusk in 35 to 40 fathoms in spring and fall. This is not a hake ground.

Old Egg Rock. This rock is WSW. from Moosabec Light, 6 miles distant, and running in a NE. and SW. direction. It is 3 miles long by 1 mile wide; has a rocky bottom and depths of 25 to 30 fathoms. This is also a small-boat ground, where fishing is done mainly by hand lines, but trawls also are employed. This ground is fished by the larger vessels in the fall months when the weather is too rough for fishing on the outside grounds. Cod, haddock, and a few pollock are taken in spring and fall; hake in fair number in the fall months.

Middle Ridge This is W. by S. from Moosabec Light 3 miles. It lies in a NE. and SW. direction and is about 1 mile long by ½ mile wide. The depths are from 18 to 25 fathoms and the bottom is rough and rocky. It is a small-boat ground mostly and of little importance as a fishing ground. Cod are present the year around haddock in late spring and summer with a smaller number in the fall. Cusk are here the year around. A few pollock are here in the spring and fall.

Broken Ground. This lies S by E from Moosabec light, 15 miles, whence the ground extends WSW to within 4 miles of Mount Desert Rock with an average width of 1 mile. The depths run from 15 to 100 fathoms. The shallows are sharp and rocky; the deeps, clay and gravel. There are places ½ mile long and others 3 miles long having depths of 70 fathoms. Several of these spots have special names: Crawley's Rocks, Puzzling Rock, The Ridges. The grounds mentioned here and those previously mentioned are known to the fishermen as the Moosabec Ridges. All these seem to be fishing spots cropping out upon the 50 fathom curve. On the Broken Ground the fishing season is from June 1 through September. Herring usually are abundant here from May to September. Cod are taken outside of the grounds in spring and fall. Pollock and small cod are taken on the shoals in summer and fall, and hake on the mud bottom in summer and fall and hake on the mud bottom in summer and fall.

Tibbetts' Ledge. This lies east from Petit Manan 4 or 5 miles. The marks are Schoodic Island over Green Island of Petit Manan and the Ladle over Nash's Island. This ledge consists of two rocky shoals with depths of 3 to 3½ fathoms, about one acre apiece in extent and 1/4 mile apart lying NW and SE from each other. To the westward of these is broken ground nearly to Petit Manan. These are favorite small-boat grounds. The eastern ledge drops suddenly into the mud. In May large cod are caught over the muddy bottom just E of the ledge in 27 to 30 fathoms. Hake and haddock are taken in late spring (May) and fall. Fishing is by hand line and trawl.

Ben's Ground. Lies ESE from Petit Manan 4 or 5 miles. The marks are Petit Manan Light to northward of Middle Hill of Mount Desert and Humpback Mountain on the west side of Trafton's Island or Pond Island Light to the eastward of Jordan's Delight. The ground is circular in shape, about 3/4 mile across, having 14 to 30 fathoms of water. The bottom is of rocks and mud. This ground is of little importance except as a small-boat ground in summer for cod and haddock. Hake are taken on the muddy bottom near it, It is a winter haddock ground in calm weather, these fish leaving it in the storms, the water being somewhat too shallow for them to "ride out a blow" in comfort, Such at least is the reason the fishermen give for the sudden cessation of their taking on shoal grounds after a period of heavy weather.

Southeast Rock. This is a ledge, nearly uncovered at low tide on its shoalest spot, SSE from Petit Manan and 4½ miles distant, The shoal portions slope toward the NE a distance of 4 miles over an irregular bottom, Depths vary from 17 to 30 fathoms, The shoals are rocky, and the deeps are muddy, Cod and haddock are taken here in May and June, hake from July to September, It is a good lobster ground, also, Fishing here is by handline and trawl operated from vessels and small boats from near-by Maine ports.

Broken Ridges aka Joe Roy Ground. This lies SSE from Petit Manan 7 miles to the center. It is 2 miles long NE and SW and one mile wide and from 27 to 33 fathoms, and the bottom of rocks and mud is very uneven, The shoalest portion is near the center. It is said to be a good cod and haddock ground, and is mainly a small boat ground, although some vessel fishing is carried on here in the spring.

Black Ledges Ground. This ground lies between Jordan's Delight and the Halibut Ledges, or Black Ledges. It is a good haddock ground for a brief season in the spring and early summer when the fish are following the herring schools. In general it is a small-boat ground on which chiefly hand lines and trawls are operated, A few cod and cusk are taken here in the fall, and it is a good lobster ground.

Bakers Island Ridge. This is a narrow ledge making out from Bakers Island E, by N. The eastern part bears S. by E. from Schoodic Island 3/4 mile distant The ridge is much broken, its average width being ½ mile, and it has depths of from 20 to 25 fathoms over a rocky and gravelly bottom. It is not much fished on the shoaler spots, but in 30 to 35 fathoms, on a muddy bottom, hake are abundant from July to October, inclusive. Cod and cusk are found here in the spring and fall; haddock from October to January, inclusive. Fishing here is done by small boats and small vessels mainly from Bass Harbor and Southwest Harbor by trawl and hand line. It is a very good lobster ground.

Martins Ground; Hillards Reef. The center bears WSW. from Schoodic Point, distant 3 miles. It is a rocky patch of 4 or 5 acres and has depths of from 15 to 25 fathoms. It is not important except for its hand-lining for cod and haddock in the spring and fall months and for hake in the fall. It is a good lobster ground.

Egg Rock Broken Ground. This is a rocky ridge making out S. by W. from Egg Rock Ledges and is about 2 miles long by 14 miles wide. It has an irregular bottom, with depths from 9 to 15 fathoms. This ridge, with Martins and Seaveys Grounds, divides the western or Bakers Island mud channel from Schoodic mud channel. Both these were formerly considered very good hake grounds but, while still good, are not as profitable for hake fishing as in past years. Haddock are taken on the ridge in the spring and in October, November, and December. A few cod are taken in the spring and fall. Fishing is by trawl and hand line. It is a good lobster ground.

Inner Schoodic Ridge. This ridge bears SE. by S. from Bakers Island, the center distant 12 miles. This ground is nearly circular in form, about 4 miles in diameter, and has depths running from 18 to 60 fathoms. The bottom is of rocks, gravel, and mud; the shoaler portions are sharp and rocky. Vessels from Maine ports use this ground, fishing by hand line and trawl. Cod and haddock are abundant here in spring and fall, and hake fishing is good through the summer. It is a good lobster ground.

Outer Schoodic Ridge. The northwest part of this ground bears SE. from Bakers Island, from which it is distant 22 miles. It lies 7 miles outside Inner Schoodic, has long been considered one of the best shore fishing grounds of the Maine coast, and still seems to deserve the reputation. The ridge is about 8 miles long in a NE. and SW. direction, lying nearly parallel with the adjacent coast. Its greatest breadth is 6 miles. The bottom is broken and irregular and has depths from 22 to 80 fathoms over rocks and gravel on the shoaler parts and mud on the deeps. Principally Maine vessels fish this ground, using hand line and trawl. Cod, pollock, haddock, cusk, and hake are present here from June to November, and a few large halibut, up to 300 pounds in weight, are taken here in June and July.

Mount Desert Outer Ridge. This ridge lies SE. by E. from the Big Hill of Mount Desert Island. From Schoodic Island to the center of this ground is about 25 miles. Its length E. by N. and W. by S, is 2 miles; its breadth 3/4 mile. Depths are from 45 to 60 fathoms; the shoals are rocky, but on the sides sand and clay predominate. This is a comparatively small ground, but it furnishes good cod fishing in the spring (April to July) and fall. Cusk are taken in the spring and fall. Virtually no haddock are taken here. Hake are found in the deep water on the W. and SW. in spring, summer, and fall; trawl lines principally are used here. It is a good lobster ground but is too distant for present fishing methods.

Flat Ground. This ground lies between Mount Desert and Swan Island, SW. from Long Island. In 50 fathoms, on a hard mud bottom, there is good fishing for hake in the summer. Fishing is by hand line and trawl.

Enoch's Shoal. This shoal lies ENE. 3 miles from Great Duck Island. This is a small hummock on the outer parts of a ridge extending out to it from Great Duck island. It has a sharp, rocky bottom with depths of about 18 fathoms. Hand lining and trawling are the methods employed to take a few cod in early spring; haddock are here in small numbers in the summer as well as a small quantity of hake. It is a good lobster ground.

Banks Ground. The center bears SE. by S. from Great Duck Island, distant about 5 miles. It is about 1½ miles long in a NE. and SW. direction by 1/4 mile wide and has a mud bottom with depths from 35 to 50 fathoms. It is mainly a small-boat ground, fished mostly in the summer, when hake are fairly abundant and there are a few haddock and cod. It is a lobster ground, also.

Shell Ground. This lies SE. from Long island Head, from which the center of the ground is distant 6 miles. It is 2 miles long, in a NE. and SW. direction and about ½ mile wide. In the middle portion is a shoal of 25 fathoms, its bottom sharp rocks. On all sides of this shoal the bottom is quite irregular, consisting of pebbles and mud. The greatest depth, near the edge of the bank, is 50 fathoms. Cod and haddock, together with a few cusk and pollock, are taken here in June, July, and August and even into the late fall, but it is mainly a hake fishing ground for small boats and an occasional larger craft, all using hand line and trawl. It is a good lobster ground.

Abner Ground. This ground is SSE. from Gott's Island, distant 8 miles. It extends 1½ miles in a NE. and SW. direction and is about 1/4 mile wide. The bottom is broken, rocks and mud, with depths of from 25 to 50 fathoms. This is principally a haddock ground, the best season being in July and August, and is resorted to mostly by small craft.

Grumpy. Extends from SE. 4½ miles from Eastern Ear of Isle au Haute to SE. 1/4 E. from the western head of Isle au Haute, distant 7 miles. This ground is 2½ miles long by 3/4 mile wide and has a small shoal of 14 fathoms on the northeast part. Over the rest of the ground the average depths run from 35 to 40 fathoms over a gravelly bottom. Though not of great importance of late years, this was formerly considered one of the best inshore grounds for cod for the entire year and for haddock in winter. Hake usually are abundant just off the southeast edge in summer. This bank is mostly fished by craft from ports of eastern Maine—small boats as a rule—and the principal method is by trawling, although there is considerable hand-lining for cod in 25 fathoms in June and July. Marks: Big Camden Mountain over the Eastern Ear of Isle au Haute; Fog Island in Jericho Bay, touching on the eastern part of Big Spoon Island; Brimstone between Isle au Haute and the Western Ear.

Hatchell Ground. This ground lies SE. by E 3/4 E. 9½ miles from the western head of Isle au Haute. Marks are eastern Mount Desert Hill in the Middle Saddle of Long island, and Little Spoon Island in the great or center Saddle of Isle au Haute.

Blue Hill Ground. This ground lies approximately E: by S. ¾ S from the western head of Isle au Haute, distant 7 miles. The bottom consists of gravel and pebbles. Marks: Brimstone Island out by the western head of Isle au Haute and Blue Hill on the west side of Marshall Island. These marks lead to a depth of 25 fathoms on the northeast part of the ground, deepening southwest to 40 fathoms in 1 mile from the shoaler part, which is about ½ mile wide, part of the ground, deepening southwest to 40 fathoms in 1 mile from the shoaler part, which is about ½ mile wide. This is a good ground for cod in the spring and fall but is best for haddock during the entire winter. Hand lines and trawl are used.

Inner Horse Reef. This reef lies SE. ¾ E 1½ miles from the eastern ear of isle au Haute. There is a shoal here of 25 fathoms about 1/8 mile in diameter. From this the water gradually deepens to NE. for ½ mile, where it drops off into the mud. Depths on this northeast portion are about 35 fathoms. The bottom is of pebbles and gravel. In spring and fall this is a good cod ground. Hake are found close to the edge in summer. Fishing is by small craft, generally, using trawl and handline. It is a good lobster ground. Marks: Bring Blue Hill Mountain in the saddle of White Horse; Brimstone showing between Western Ear and Isle au Haute.

Outer Horse Reef. This is a short distance SW. from the Inner Reef, with only a narrow gully between. The small shoal falls off rapidly on all sides. It has a depths of 30 fathoms. Over a space 1/4 mile in diameter the bottom is gravelly. Seasons and species are as on Inner Horse Reef.

Hake Ground. North of Monhegan island lies a patch called the Hake Ground or Mud Channel, the first name because of the abundance of hake taken here during June, July, and August. It extends from just outside White Head to abreast of Monhegan Island on the northern side. The depths vary from 20 to 45 fathoms, and the ground is still considered one of the best hake grounds alongshore. It is fished by small boats and vessels when the dogfish are on the outer grounds. This is a good haddock ground in December and January, as well as a good lobster ground.

Southwest Ground. This lies 2 miles SW. from the western head of Isle au Haute. It is circular in form, ½ mile in diameter and has a gravelly bottom with depths varying from 35 to 40 fathoms. It is a cod ground from April to June and from September to November, inclusive. A few pollock and haddock are taken with the cod. Hake are abundant in summer close to Isle au Haute. Handlines and trawls are used in the fishing. It is also a good lobster ground.

Barley Hill Ground. This ground lies NNE. from Seal Island and SSW from the western head of Isle au Haute directly in line between the two, about 3½ miles distant from each point. It is circular in form, has 28 to 30 fathoms of water, and the bottom is mixed mud and rocks. This is a ground much resorted to by sloops and larger vessels, and the fishing is by hand line and trawls. It is a good cod ground in spring and fall and a hake ground on the mud and rocks in summer. Occasionally a few halibut are taken here during June and July. It is also a lobster ground.

Gilkey Ground. This bears S. from the western head of Isle au Haute. 4 miles distant. It extends ENE. and WSW about 1½ miles long by 1/3 mile wide. The bottom is rocky on the shoals where depths are about 23 fathoms sloping to 35 fathoms on the southwest part., where the bottom is gravelly and comparatively smooth.

This is a cod ground in spring and fall, a haddock ground in winter, and hake are taken on the edges in summer. Vessels fishing here are mostly from Maine ports. It is also a good lobster ground.

Rock Cod Ledge. This ledge lies NE. of Seal Island 1 mile. It has a depth of 3½ fathoms on the shoalest part, deepening gradually on all sides for a considerable distance. The bottom is of sharp rocks and is broken in places. Rock cod area present in fair numbers in spring and fall, and this is a mackerel and herring ground in their seasons. Haddock are abundant in the fall close in to the rocks of Seal Island in 6 to 15 fathoms. This is not a hake ground, although there are a few cusk to be had here on the deeper parts and an occasional small halibut is taken in the kelp on the shoal in June and July. It is a good lobster ground.

Gravel Bottom and Southeast Ground. These lie S. of Seal Island. forming an extensive piece of fairly level ground extensive piece of fairly level ground. The western that bears a little E. of S. and the eastern part about ESE. from the island. It is about 5 or 10 miles in diameter. While this is really but one piece of ground, the eastern part is called the Southeast Ground and the western part, from the nature of its bottom.

The Gravel Bottom. The eastern portion is muddy and has 40 to 60 fathoms. The western has 35 to 40 fathoms. It is a good cod ground in winter and spring. Haddock are present from November to March, inclusive; hake in summer. Fishing is done mainly by trawling by sloops and vessels.

Laisdells Ground. This is a small, rocky spot outside the Brandy Ledges. It is about 1/4 acre in extent and has a sharp rocky bottom with 20 fathoms of water over it. It is the best cod and haddock ground in Isle au Haute Bay. This is chiefly a small boat ground and is also a lobster ground.

Saddleback Reef. This reef lies S. from Saddle-back Ledge, 3/4 mile distant. It is about 2/3 mile long N and S by 1/4 mile wide. Depths are from 15 to 35 fathoms over a broken and rocky bottom. Cod are taken here by hand line in May and June; haddock and cod by trawling in fall and winter (November to January 1). It is a good lobster ground and chiefly a small-boat ground.

Otter Island Reef; Snipper Shin; Western Reef. These are names applied to different sections of an irregular, broken piece of rocky ground about halfway between Vinalhaven and Seal Island. Otter Island Reef is the eastern section, lying 4 miles W. by S. by 1/4 S. from the western head of Isle au Haute. Depths here are from 10 to 25 fathoms over a rocky bottom. The trawl, formerly not much used here, is now in general use. This is a cod and haddock ground at seasons when these fish are in shoal water, but it is best for cod in winter and spring and for haddock in the fall, from November 1 to January 1.

Old Ripper. This lies S. from the Western Ground (Western Reef) and 10 miles WSW. from Criehaven or Ragged Island. Apparently this is a part of the Western Ground. On the deep-water mud bottom between these (Ripper and Western Reef) is good hake fishing in summer, and cusk are abundant from May to the time when the dogfish strike the ground, usually about July 5 to 10.

Crie Ridges. These lie 4 miles NW. from Matinicus Rock, 4 miles WSW. from Criehaven or Ragged Island, and run SE. from Western Ground toward Matinicus, distant 4½ to 5 miles. Cod, pollock, and cusk are here in the spring, and haddock are abundant in the fall.

Bald Ridges. These begin just outside Wooden Ball Island and run off in a nearly direct line for Matinicus Rock. They are each from ¼ to ½ mile wide, are quite close together, the distances between them being not over ½ mile, and they are almost parallel with each other. Soundings show from 15 to 30 fathoms upon them, with a broken, rocky bottom. The shoalest water is about 1 mile from Wooden Ball Island, the depth increasing toward the southern end.

This is a good cod ground at all times when the fish are on the coast, the spring school being the largest. The shoal is a favorite place for rock cod. Haddock are present from January 1 to February 15. Hake are abundant in their season on the mud bottom inside the Bald Ridges 1½ miles WSW, in 50 fathoms. It is a good lobster ground.

Henry Marshalls Ground. This ground lies S. by W. from Matinicus Rock about 3 miles; its area is about 2 acres. The shoaler portion has a depth of 35 fathoms and a gravelly bottom; on the edge the depth is 45 fathoms and the bottom is of rocks and mud. Cod are taken here in the spring, haddock in January and February, and hake in the summer months. It is a good lobster ground.

The Bounties (The Bowdies). This ground bears SE. by S ½ S distant 6 miles from Wooden Ball Island. It is nearly circular in form, about 4 miles across, and has depths from 40 to 60 fathoms. The bottom, of gravel and rocks, is somewhat broken. It is a good cod and cusk ground in spring and fall and a haddock ground in winter and is fished by vessels and sloops, mainly by trawling but with a certain amount of hand lining, in May and June. A summer hake ground extends from 3 miles ESE. of Seal Island to 4 miles SSE of the Wooden Ball, thus it is about 7½ miles long by some 2½ miles wide. The depths here are from 35 to 60 fathoms.

Summer Hake Ground. A summer hake ground extends from 8 miles SE. of the eastern Ear of Isle au Haute to 3 miles SE. of Long Island in 35 to 60 fathoms on a bottom of hard mud. This piece of ground is about 15 miles long by 4 miles wide.

Minerva Hub. This bears SSE. from Matinicus Rock, distant 6 miles. This is a small, gravelly spot about 1/4 mile in diameter and with a depth of 35 fathoms, abounding with cod in spring and fall. It is a summer ground for hake and cusk. Hand lines and trawls are used.

Haddock Nubble. This lies SE. ½ S. from Matinicus Rock, distant 16 miles, and has an average depth of 50 fathoms over a small, circular patch some 2,000 feet across. The bottom is of gravel and rocks, and "lemons" and marine growths of like nature are abundant. This is a June cod ground, usually furnishing good haddocking, also, from November to January, inclusive.

Skate Bank. This bank bears SSE. from Matinicus Rock, distant 12 miles. It is about 2 miles in diameter and nearly circular in form. Depths are from

35 to 60 fathoms. The bottom is gravelly but quite uneven. The best season on this ground for cod and cusk is from April to July. Hake abound in July and August. Hand lines and trawls are used here, fished by sloops and vessels.

Matinicus Sou'Sou'West Grounds. These grounds bear SSW. from Matinicus Rock, from which the inner edge of the grounds is distant 6 miles. They extend about 9 miles N. and S. and have about the same width, being nearly triangular in shape, broadest at the northern end. On the northern part there is a shoal of about 30 fathoms 2 miles long E. and W. and 1 mile wide. Sharp rocks cover this, but the ground is not broken and drops off gradually to depths of 50 to 55 fathoms or even to 60 fathoms on the southern part. Outside of the shoal the bottom is pebbly and gravelly. This is one of the best cod and haddock grounds in the vicinity. Cod are sometimes abundant here all winter; haddock are found here from December 1 to February and are more abundant than the cod. Hake are plentiful on this ground and in 60 fathoms on the mud off the edge SE. of this ground during the summer season. Marks: The high pinnacle on the eastern end of Wooden Ball, showing just out by Matinicus Rock, SW. by S. from the rock, 5 miles.

Inner Breaker. This lies 2 miles W. of the southwest point of Matinicus Island. It is a rocky shoal about 1 acre in extent and having 7 fathoms of water. From this shoal the bottom slopes gradually to depths of 25 to 30 fathoms, and this slope furnishes good fishing for cod in May and June, while haddock are here in December and January. A good school of hake is found on the edge of the ground in summer. The bottom is rocky and broken and, while sharp, is fished with trawls as well as hand lines. It is mostly a small-boat ground.

Towhead Grounds. These grounds hear N. by E. ½ E. from Matinicus Island, from which they are distant 2½ miles. Depths are from 12 to 30 fathoms. It is somewhat irregular in shape and has a very rocky, broken bottom. The ground is from 2½ to 3 miles long and ½ to 1½ miles wide. It extends E. by S. and W. by N. and is considered one of the best inside shoal grounds for cod and haddock in the bay. Hand lines and trawls are used here now, although in former times this and the preceding grounds were considered too sharp for the use of trawls. Both these are good lobster grounds and chiefly small-boat grounds.

Green Island Ridge (or Western Ridge) and the Pigeon Ground. The northern portion of this ridge lies 6½ miles NW. by W. from Matinicus Rock, from which the ground extends about 7 miles in a SSW. direction. The greatest width is not over 1 mile. Depths are from 15 to 30 fathoms.

The bottom is broken and rocky. It is a good cod ground in the spring and fall. Haddock are found here in June, November, and December. In summer this is a good hake ground. Halibut are found on the shoals (10 fathoms) and about the northern part of Western Green Island, on the sandy bottom during June and July.

Matinic Bank. This is an extension of the shore soundings that make out to the southward and eastward of Matinic a distance of 2 or 3 miles, with depths (outside of 1½ miles) of 23 to 30 fathoms. The bottom is level, consisting of rocks, pebbles, and gravel, and the ground abounds in cod in the season from March to June. Just off the edge, in depths of from 40 to 50 fathoms, the bottom is soft mud, on which hake abound in summer. Very few haddock are taken on this bank. Halibut are sometimes abundant here in 10 to 15 fathoms during May and June.

Matinic Ooze. This is a flat bottom, composed of ooze and shells, that makes off to the eastward of the Haddock Ledge and Shoal and bears about S. from Matinic. The Haddock Shoal and the Ooze are really parts of one ground, though they have been given different names by the fishermen. The Haddock Shoal (3 miles S. by B. from the Seal Ledge: breaks in rough weather) is thought to be poor ground and is but little fished, although it is a fall haddock ground. The Ooze falls off gradually, reaching a depth of 50 fathoms on the outer part. It is considered fair fishing ground for cod and haddock in the spring and for cod and hake in the summer and fall.

Freemans Ground. This ground lies 6½ miles E. from Monhegan Island between Ornes Ground and Matinicus Western Ground. It is 3 miles long and 1 mile wide and runs in a NE. and SW. direction. There is a shoal on the southwest part having 20 fathoms over a sharp rocky bottom. The rest of the ground has depths of 25 to 40 fathoms, the bottom of rocks, gravel, and shells, in some places uneven and in others smooth. This is a good spring ground for cod and for cod, hake, and pollock in the fall. Haddock are not numerous on this ground, though a few are usually to be found here in December. Herring are here May to August.

Middle Shoal, Pollock Rip, Allens Shoal, and Deckers Shoal. These are small rocky patches lying to eastward of Monhegan Island and northerly from the Outer Shoal. They have depths from 6 to 30 fathoms over a sharp, rocky, and broken bottom. Middle Shoal is 2 miles from the island. Pollock Rip 1½ miles. Allens Shoal 1 1/4 miles, having 5½ fathoms and breaking in rough weather; and Deckers Shoal 1 mile. Depths vary here from 6 to 30 fathoms over a bottom generally sharp and rocky. The principal fishing here is hand-lining for cod in the spring during the herring season and in the fall in "squid time". A few pollock are taken here also.

A number of small patches lie westerly from the Outer Shoal and close to Monhegan Island. These are the Cusk Ground with a depth of 20 to 35 fathoms; Gull Rock Ledge (breaks in rough weather) 3½ fathoms; Lobster Point Ground, 15 to 30 fathoms; Inner Spring Ground, 15 to 30 fathoms; Outer Spring Ground 25 to 30 fathoms. All these are fished for cod nearly all the year, for haddock in December and January, and for pollock in early spring and late fall. The Spring Grounds are near the harbor and so are fished before the others. All are lobster grounds. Small boats and vessels operate here.

Black Island Ground. This ground is ENE. 2 miles from Monhegan. 1 mile in diameter, has a shoal of 10 fathoms, and sharp rocky bottom in the center. The ground slopes gradually from this to the edges, where are 40 fathoms. Beyond the depths of 28 to 30 fathoms the bottom is gravelly and smoother. This is a cod ground in spring, and cod and hake are taken here on the edges in summer and fall. Pollock are found about the shoal in summer. It is a good lobster ground.

Franklin Ground. This ground is NE. by N. midway between Monhegan and Burnt Island, distant 4 miles. Cod and haddock are found here from April to June and pollock in summer. In summer and fall hake are taken by night fishing with hand line about the rocks in 20 to 30 fathoms on the broken ground. Fishing here is by hand-lining in summer and trawling in fall and winter. It is a lobster ground.

White Head Ground. Depths on the shoal (the White Hub: Bring Budd cottage out by White Head, Black Head. and Allens Island touching) are 7 fathoms, thence to 20 fathoms on the edges about it. This ground extends NE. and SW., 2 miles long by 1/4 mile wide. The bottom is chiefly broken, of rocks, and with spots of coarse gravel and sand. Fish and their seasons are as on Franklin Ground. Marks: Bring Black Head, White Head, and Gull Head in range on the east side of Monhegan Island.

Burnt Island, Inner Ridge aka Andrews Shoal. This is NE. by E. from Monhegan, distant 5 miles. It is a broken ground with depths from 15 to 20 fathoms, the bottom rocky and gravelly, with occasional mud holes. It extends NE. about 4 miles, nearly to Roaring Bull Ledge, and is ½ mile wide. There are strong tidal currents here, the flood being NE., the ebb SW. It is a cod ground from April to June, and cod and hake are taken from September to November; haddock in December. It is a good lobster ground.

Burnt Island, Outer Ridge. This ground is parallel with the Inner Ridge and at a distance of 3/4 mile. Depths are from 5 to 25 fathoms, the bottom being rather less broken than on the Inner Ridge. Fishing seasons and species are as on Inner Ridge. Hand-lining is done mostly because of strong tides. It is a good lobster ground.

Ornes Ground. This ground bears E., distant 4½ miles from Monhegan Light to the center. It is 1 mile long. E. and W. and 1 mile wide. Depths are from 30 to 45 fathoms. On the shoal parts the bottom is of sharp rocks and broken. On other parts it is generally pebbly and quite level. The shoal lies toward the eastern part of the ground and is a good spring cod ground; also a pollock ground in the spring and fall. It is a night fishing ground for hake, by hand lining close to the rocks during September and October. Herring are abundant here usually in May and June. It is a good lobster ground. Fishing is done by hand lines and trawls.

Outer Shoal. This ground is ESE from Monhegan Light about 2½ miles. It is circular in form and about 1½ miles across. Depths are from 10 to 38 fathoms. There is a small rocky shoal in the center of the ground; the remainder of this piece has a gravelly bottom. This is a cod ground from spring to fall and a good pollock ground in September. A few haddock are taken here about the edges in December. Hake are abundant on the edges on the mud in 45 to 50 fathoms during the spring, summer and fall.

Monhegan Inner Sou'Southeast Ground. This ground is SSE from Monhegan Light. It is circular in form and 1/14 miles across. The center is 5 miles fro the light. Depths are from 30 to 50 fathoms, the shoalest water being on the eastern part, the shoal has a broken and rocky bottom, but the rest of the ground is gravelly and muddy. The principal fishes taken are cod and cusk in the spring, summer and fall. Very few haddock are found here. Pollock are numerous in the fall, when they are taken by hand lining. Hake are abundant in September and October. June is the best fishing month, except when the squid strike the ground in the fall. This is mainly a small boat ground, fished by trawls, hand lines and an increasing number of gill nets.

Monhegan Outer Sou'Southeast. Three miles outside the Inner Ground on the same bearing and similar in size and form. The bottom is rocky and muddy or of hard clay. The depths are from 35 to 55 fathoms. The same species are found here as on Inner Sou'Southeast and at the same seasons, and in addition, hand lining is done for cod in August and September.

Blue Ground. This is SE 1½ E from Monhegan, distant 14 miles; E 1½ S from Portland Lightship 45 miles, and SW from Matinicus Rock 9 miles to southern Edge. Fishermen usually take the Monhegan bearing [12] for their starting point. This ground has a small shoal in the center, having 28 to 30 fathoms, from which the bottom slopes off to 45 and 60 fathoms on the edges. The shoal is broken and rocky, bu the deep water is over a level gravelly bottom. This ground is circular in form and about 2 miles across. It is both a small-boat and vessel ground, larger craft operating here mainly in the fall. Hake are found here in large numbers in summer and fall; cusk are taken in the deep water the year around but are most abundant in January. Cod are here the year around, the largest school occurring in February and March.

Monhegan Southeast Ground. This ground lies SE from Monhegan Island, the center distant 12 miles. This is nearly circular, 3 miles in diameter. The bottom is so broken that depths may vary much within a short distance, but depths are from 35 to 75 fathoms over a bottom of rocks, gravel and mud. Fishing is by trawl and handline. It is good cod ground from April to July; haddock are taken in December and hake in summer on the edges in 50 to 60 fathoms.

Hill Ground. This ground is SSW 9 miles from Matinic: between 3 and 4 miles long NE and SW and some 2 miles wide. The shoalest part has 35 fathoms and a rocky bottom. From this it slopes gradually to a depth of 50 fathoms over a bottom of mixed gravel, rocks and mud. Its best fishing is for hake, using both hand lines and trawls.

Monhegan Inner Sou'Sou'west Ground. this ground takes its name from its bearing, lying SSW from Monhegan light, distant 5 miles. Its width is 1½ miles, its length NNE and SSW is 1 1/4 miles. It has a sharp, broken, rocky bottom, including a small shoal of 20 fathoms and some hummocks of rather greater depths. The deepest water is in the neighborhood of 50 fathoms. Fishing here is from May until July for codfish and pollock: hake and cusk are in the deep water in the spring months and halibut on the shoal in July and September. This ground is principally fished by trawls, but there is considerable hand lining in September and October. Gillnetting, too, has become more common of later years.

Harris Ground. From 15 miles S ½ W from Monhegan island to 6 miles SSW. It has 40 to 50 fathoms over a bottom of sharp rocks and mud—a "blistery" bottom. Cod, cusk and hake are found here the year around. Halibut are here in June, July and August. Fishing is by trawling and hand lining, with very little gillnetting.

The 45 Fathom Bunch. Sixteen miles S 1½ E from Monhegan. This is a great ground for June hand lining for cod. Thence 1 mile ENE to 70 fathom depth, which leads to a piece of ground leading to the Inner Fall, on which, on a hard bottom and mud where there is an abundance of "lemons" and similar forms, are found cod cusk and pollock in June. The ground is about 6 miles long, WSW and ENE by 1 mile wide.

Another Forty Five Fathom Bunch lies 22 miles S ½ E from Monhegan. This ground is 4 miles long by 1 mile wide, running ENE and WSW, and has depths from 45 to 75 fathoms. This is likewise a great cod hand lining ground in June.

Another of the same name lies 26 miles S 1½ E from Monhegan. It has a 49 fathom shoal and the species and seasons are much the same as on the other grounds of the name. This is probably the ground known to other vessel captains as Toothaker Ridge.

Monhegan Outer Sou'Sou'West. This ground is SSW from Monhegan Light. the center distant 9 miles It is 4 miles long, NNE and SSW and about 2 miles wide, and has 45 fathoms on the shoalest part but the depths generally are from 60 to 80 fathoms. The bottom generally is gravelly and quite level. The ground is fished by both boats and vessels using hand lines and trawls.

This is a cod ground in spring and fall. In summer hake are abundant here, and halibut are quite plentiful in July on the shoalest part.

Old Jeffrey. An exceedingly good ground. It is said that better fishing may be had here than on any other ground of its size in the vicinity. This piece of bottom bears SE from Pumpkin Rock, from which the center is distant about 6 miles. It is about 3 miles long NE and SW, and about 1 mile wide. The bottom is broken, of gravel and mud, with depths from 25 to 50 fathoms. Fishing here is by trawling and land-lining. In spring cod are most abundant, in late summer and fall hake, cod, and pollock are taken. Halibut are found on the shoaler parts in July.

Little Jeffrey. A small piece of broken, rocky bottom, roughly circular in form. Depths average 35 fathoms. Species and seasons are as on Old Jeffrey, from which it lies about 4 miles NE by E.

Monhegan Western Ground. This is a somewhat extensive ground lying about 4½ miles WSW from Monhegan Island. The depths range from 22 to 45 fathoms. Its length is 4 or 5 miles, and its greatest breadth is 2 miles on the eastern portion, gradually narrowing westward to about 1 mile. The ground runs SE and NW. Pollock are found here in September and October. It is fished by hand lines, trawls and gill nets. Marks: Bring houses on New Harbor over the white cliff on Pemaquid 6 miles from New Harbor.

Broken Ground. The center bears nearly S. from Pumpkin Island (at entrance to Boothbay Harbor), distant 7 miles. It extends 4 miles in an ENE. and WSW direction and has an average width of 1¾ miles. Depths are from 35 to 50 fathoms on a bottom of rocks and mud. Cod are taken here the year around; hake from June to September. Cusk also are found here all the year in 40 fathoms depths. It is fair herring ground on spring nights.

Great Ledge. Ten miles S. from Cape Newagen. It is about 4 miles long, SSW. and NNE and from 1 to 2 miles wide. There is said to be a shoal of 14 fathoms on the northern edge and another of 22 fathoms near the center. These are both broken and rocky, but the main part of the ground, having depths of 30 to 45 fathoms, is mostly composed of sand. is quite level, and slopes gradually toward the edge. It is a good ground for cod and haddock in winter and for cod in the spring. A few pollock are taken here, also. Halibut are found on the shoals in July. On these, also, are good lobster grounds. It is chiefly a small-boat and vessel ground, fishing being done by hand lines and trawls, with some gill netting. Marks: Show the sawtooth of Morse's Mountain coming out by Seguin on the western side; hold this until Pumpkin Island comes onto White Island.

Barnum Head Grounds. These lie SSE. from Damariscove Island and are about 1 mile long by 400 yards wide. Depths are from 40 to 70 fathoms over broken ground of sharp rocks on the shoals, with mud on the deeper parts. This ground is fished by hand lines, gill nets, and trawls mainly by boats and small craft. Cod, haddock, and pollock are found here in the spring and fall months: hake in the muddy parts in summer. It is a summer hand-line ground for cod and pollock also. Marks: Bring the peak of Heron Island on Damariscove and the "Whistler" on Seguin, 7 miles from Damariscove Island (this gives 21-fathom soundings) or Big White Island's inner part just touching on Barnum Head; Morse Mountain (in Kennebec) touching on eastern part of Seguin to make a sawtooth.

Peterson's Ground. Lies distant SW. from Monhegan 20 miles and SSE. from Seguin 16 miles. This is about 3 miles long in an ENE. and WSW. direction by about 1½ miles wide. The northern and western edges rise sharply from the 85 or 90 fathoms of the muddy bottom about it to 60 fathoms over a bottom of rocks and stones. Easterly and southerly the ground slopes away gradually over hard gravel to 90 fathoms. Cod and hake furnish the best fishing here—at its peak during October and November.

Cusk Ridge. It lies S. ½ E. 12 miles from Pumpkin Island, 3½ to 4 miles long, NE. and SW., and 1/4 mile wide. This ground is somewhat difficult to find. It has a bottom of black gravel and rocks with 30 to 60 fathoms of water over it. A "blistery" bottom that is a cod ground the year around, the best of the fishing occurring in the spring months. Hake are abundant in the fall, and cusk fishing is exceptionally good in the deep water in June.

Potato Patch. Three miles WNW. from Monhegan. A round nubble about 14 mile in diameter, of sharp, rocky bottom having about 40 fathoms over it. Cusk and cod are taken on the shoal and hake from the muddy edges about it.

The Apron. Four and one-half miles from Monhegan. Marks are the tripod on Eastern Egg Rock over Franklin Island Light; Monhegan Light over the middle of Manana. Its length is 5 miles and its width 3 miles. It is a broken piece of ground with 10 to 45 fathoms. Cod are present the year around and haddock all the year except for a few weeks in summer. Cusk are here most of the year, but the season for pollock is September.

Henry Gallant Ridges. The inner one lies 16½ miles S. by E. of Monhegan Island, extending in a NNE. and SSW. direction, about 1 mile long by 1/4 mile wide. The outer ridge lies about 1¼ miles farther from the island on the same bearing as the first and paralleling it and apparently is about the same size. The bottom on both shoals is of gravel and black rocks with depths averaging 45 fathoms but rising from the 80 and 90 fathoms of the surrounding muddy ground. Both these are year-around cod grounds, the spring months, however, having The largest school. Cusk also are abundant on both shoals in the spring.

Mosers Ledge, also known as Middle Ground. This piece of shoal ground lies about midway between Monhegan Island and Pemaquid and has a 3-fathom shoal on the eastern part where the sea breaks in heavy weather. This shoal, called Mosers Ledge, is broken and rocky but slopes gradually to the SW., reaching 48 fathoms, with a bottom of gravel and mud on the deepest part. The ground is about 2 miles long NE. and SW. and about 1 mile wide. It is good ground for cod and haddock in the spring and for herring in June and other top-schooling fish In their season. Mackerel occur in late August and September. It is a lobster ground the year around.

Johns Head Ground. About 4 miles SSE. from Pemaquid Point. Depths are from 25 to 15 fathoms over a sandy bottom, making a good cod ground in April and May. The ground is of circular form about 1 mile in diameter. Hand lines and trawls, together with some gill nets, are used on the sand shoal.

White Island Ground. This is ESE from White Island, from which its inner edge is distant ¼ mile and the outer edge about 4 miles. Of triangular outline, it is widest at the outer end. It is very broken and uneven and has depths from 6 to 30 fathoms. In some places the bottom is gravelly, but on the shoal it is sharp, broken rocks. The small, rocky spots are known by other names, such as Browns Head Ground (a herring ground in June), where the fishermen catch a few rock cod. The sandy bottom furnishes good fares of haddock in May and June. "Bobber trawling" is the usual method used here in June. This ground is fished mainly by small boats and sloops using hand lines and trawls.

Steamboat Ground. Seven miles WSW. from Monhegan Island; it is 3 miles long, NE. and SW, and ½ mile wide. Its bottom is broken with patches of rocks. Depths are from 25 to 50 fathoms, the shoalest 20 fathoms. This is fished by hand lines and trawls mainly by craft from New Harbor. Cod are found here the year around but are most abundant in the fall. Haddock are present all the spring and fall; hake through the summer months; pollock in the fall. Cusk are most abundant in the spring. A certain amount of lobster fishing is done here.

Inner and Outer Boutens (Bootlegs). The inner ground lies 3 miles SW. from Monhegan Island. It is about 1 mile long. NE. and SW., by 1/4 mile wide. It has a sharp, rocky bottom, shoalest in the center, where are 25 fathoms, sloping gradually southwest and falling off suddenly on the northeast side to the mud in 60 fathoms on the edges. Cod, haddock, and cusk are here the year around. Hake occur in summer on the muddy edges. It is a fairly good lobster ground on the shoal. The Outer Bouten lies ½ mile SW. of the Inner, separated from it by a deep, muddy channel. It has a small shoal of 30 fathoms rising suddenly from the surrounding mud. Fish and seasons of their presence are as on Inner Bouten. Fishing on these grounds is mainly by hand line and trawl. Marks: The Tripod on Western Duck Island on the eastern side of the big eastern mountain of Camden: Black Head just out by White Head; White Head through the "Hole in the Wall."

Hill Ground. This ground is SSW 9 miles from Matinic: between 3 and 4 miles long NE and SW and some 2 miles wide. The shoalest part has 35 fathoms and a rocky bottom. From this it slopes gradually to a depth of 50 fathoms over a bottom of mixed gravel, rocks and mud. Its best fishing is for hake, using both hand lines and trawls.

Seguin Sou'Sou'West Ground. This ground lies SSW. from the western part of Seguin Island, the center distant 4 miles. It is a rocky shoal, ½ mile long by 200 yards wide, with a ½-acre shoal in the center. Depths are 7 to 14 fathoms. This is evidently a SSW continuation of the Hill Ground. It is fished by small boats for rock cod by hand-lining. Trawling is done in March for cod, and this is also a cod ground in April. It is both a small-boat and a vessel ground and is a lobster ground the year around. Marks: Elwells Rock touching the western side of Seguin, and Fullers Rock touching the southern part of Bald Head.

Seguin Ridge. This ridge is SSW. from Seguin Island, distant 5 miles. Four miles long. ESE. and WSW by ½ mile wide. There are a number of small rocky spots—hummocks of 9 to 14 fathoms in depth. In general the ground has from 10 to 40 fathoms over it, except as mentioned. Cod and cusk are taken in the spring, haddock in May and June. and hake in summer. It is a good cod ground in the fall and also a lobster ground. A few pollock are seined here in the spring. Fishing is by hand lines, gill netting, and trawling. Marks: Pond Island Light on the eastern spur of Seguin; Wooded Mark Island on Bald Head (Small Point).

Seguin Ground. This ground is SW. by S. from Seguin Island, distant about 7 miles to the center. About 4 miles long. NE. and SW., and a little more than 2 miles wide in the widest part. There is a small hummock called Bumpers Island Ground on the northern end with depths of 13 fathoms. The northern part is mostly rocky, but toward the south the bottom is gravelly and sloping, so that on the middle and southern portions there are depths of 35 to 45 fathoms. Cod, hake, and pollock are the principal fishes taken here and furnish some of the best fishing in this vicinity. Haddock are not common here but are abundant on the sandy bottom to the westward in April and May. Trawl fishing and gill netting are done in the spring for cod and hand lining for cod and pollock in October. It is a small-boat and vessel ground and a winter lobster ground.

McIntire Reef. This reef is SSW. from Bald Head (Cape Small Point). The distance to the center is 4½ miles. This is 2 miles long. NE. and SW., by ½ mile wide. Marks are Yarmouth Island Hill over Mark Island and Pond Island Light on the northern part of Fullers Rock. This reef is very broken and hummocky and has a rocky bottom and depths from 14 to 20 fathoms. A shoal of 7 fathoms is on the northwest part, where there is good hand-lining for cod. It is a good lobster ground. Just east of this ground is a piece of bottom composed of hard mud and shells where hake usually are abundant in summer.

Seguin Hub. This lies SSE. 5½ miles from Seguin Light. There is a collection of half a dozen small hummocks rising from the 65 or 70 fathoms of the surrounding muddy bottom to 30 or 35 fathoms of rocky bottom. These are hand-line spots. Species and seasons are as on Seguin Ground, except that a great proportion of hake are taken here on mud from 60 fathoms down. It is a cod ground in spring and summer. Marks: Hunnewell Point Woods on Seguin; Damariscotta Hill over Damariscove Island.

Cow Ground. Nearly SW. from Bald Head, the center distant 6½ miles. This is nearly 4 miles long in a NE. and SW. direction and 1½ miles wide. The northeast portion is rough and rocky and has depths from 16 to 18 fathoms. On the southwest part gravel and stones predominate, and the bottom slopes off to 20 or 30 fathom depths. Trawling and hand-lining are the principal methods employed here, but there is an increasing amount of gill netting. Cod and pollock are the principal fishes taken here, mainly in the spring. This is a lobster ground from November to April.

Murre Hub. This lies WSW. from Small Point, the center distant 10 3/4 miles and 3 miles SW. from Seguin. This ground is 3 miles long. N. and S., with an average width of 1½ miles. Depths are from 34 to 45 fathoms. The inner parts are shoalest, and the bottom there is sharp rocks and broken ground. From this the ground slopes gradually to the south, where the bottom is sand and gravel. Cod are here from spring to October; hake from June to October; and haddock are present during the winter season. Fishing is almost entirely by trawling.

Mistaken Ground. This ground bears N. from the center of New Ledge. from which it is distant about 10 miles; from Portland Lightship SE. ½ S 21 miles to the edge and 22 miles to the shoal water. It is 8 miles long in an E. and W. direction and 5 miles wide. Depths are from 45 to 100 fathoms, both the shoalest and the deepest soundings being on the western part, where the bottom is mostly rocks and boulders. There is said to be a small shoal "peak" of 35 fathoms here. Over the greater part of the ground the bottom is of rocks and gravel. In proportion to its size this ground is nearly as important as New Ledge, being resorted to by the same species of fish at the same seasons and being visited by the same type of craft, with a larger number of the small crafts operating here and the larger vessels fishing here principally during the worst of the winter weather.

The fishing is by hand line, trawl, and gill netting, with a lessening use of the hand line and an increase in the use of this ground by the gill-net fleet. Cod and cusk are taken here from May to July and through October and November, the cod predominating on the ridgy bottom in the deep water, on the western and northwestern side. Hake are also found here in the winter. Haddock are fairly abundant from December to March. There are usually many pollock on the shoal in fall and winter.

Tag Ground. Between Broken Ground and Seguin Island, ESE. from Seguin, distant 5 miles. A narrow rocky ridge 2 miles long, in a NNE. and SSW. direction, with an uneven bottom and depths from 14 to 30 fathoms. Principally a summer small-boat ground fished by hand lines, trawls, and gill nets. Cod are found here the year around. Haddock are abundant in the winter, hake in the summer months, and the pollock are here also in the summer season when "top schooling." Cusk are found in the deep water all the year.

Outer Kettle, also known as Kettle Bottom. The center of this ground bears S. from Seguin Island, from which the northern edge of the ground is distant 10 miles. Its length is 12 miles in a N. and S. direction, and its width 10 miles, thus being roughly circular in forum. It is an uneven piece of bottom consisting of rocks, gravel, and mud. The depths range from 25 to

75 fathoms. This is one of the best fishing grounds on this part of the coast. Cod are the most abundant fish and are taken the year around. Haddock are plentiful in the winter months and cusk are present all the year in the 50-fathom depths. Fishing here is by trawl, hand line, and gill nets operated by small boats, sloops, and, in the rougher weather of the winter, larger vessels, which visit it also, generally to make one "set" at a season when a "fish day" (one on which it is possible to fish) is the exception.

Murray Hole. A small circular piece of ground about 1½ miles across and capable of taking about 40 or 50 lines of trawl: it lies between the two kettles and heads S. by E. from Seguin. Depths here are from 42 to 60 fathoms over a bottom of pebbles and gravel. It is a good cod and hake ground in June and July.

Inner Kettle. This is S. by E. from Seguin and distant 8 miles. The depths here average 40 fathoms over a bottom of gravel and rocks. Species and season of abundance are as on the Outer Kettle. Marks are as follows: The Eastern Hawkwings (west side of the Kennebec River) on western side of Seguin; Damariscove Mountain just touching the east side of Damariscove Island.

Bantam. This ground lies off Seguin 6 miles E. by N. It has a bottom of rocky broken ground. There is a buoy in the center over a reef that is said to break at low water. Elsewhere depths range from 14 to 20 fathoms. The shoal is about 2 miles long in a NE. and SW. direction and is about 1 mile wide. This is a cod and haddock ground in the spring, and bake are plentiful in summer on the edges of the ground.

White Head Ground. Depths on the shoal (the White Hub: Bring Budd cottage out by White Head, Black Head. and Allens Island touching) are 7 fathoms, thence to 20 fathoms on the edges about it. This ground extends NE. and SW., 2 miles long by 1/4 mile wide. The bottom is chiefly broken, of rocks, and with spots of coarse gravel and sand. Fish and their seasons are as on Franklin Ground. Marks: Bring Black Head, White Head, and Gull Head in range on the east side of Monhegan Island.

Green Ground. This is a hand-line spot for cod all the year, but the fishing is best in the spring and continues good until the last of the fishing for cod about the river mouths in June. There are two shoals, one of 14 and the other of 16 feet, both of which break in rough weather, but depths elsewhere on the ground about are from 13 to 20 fathoms. The bottom, both on the shoals and about them, is rocky and has many starfish upon it, except on the north-western part, where the bottom is of sand. Marks: The eastern end of Elmwood Rock on the little high woods of Small Point: the Outer Sister on Lower Five Island.

Lambo. This lies B. by N. from Halfway Rock 5 miles. It has a buoy upon it, marking a 5 fathom shoal that breaks in heavy weather. Good fishing is to be had in all directions about it, with haddock in June on the sand outside it, hake inside in August, and cod on the hard bottom about it; but for these it is mostly a summer hand-line spot.

Bull Ground. This is an irregularly shaped piece of bottom of indefinite area, being perhaps 3 miles long by 2 miles wide. It lies between Lambo Ledge and the White Bull and at about 2 miles distance from Ragged Island. The bottom here is of rocks and mud with depths from 20 to 30 fathoms. This ground furnishes hake fishing in June, July, and August. Cod are taken here in good numbers in the fall by gill nets, with a lesser amount also in the spring by the same method. In the winter the cod are taken here by "bobber trawl." Haddock are taken about the edges in August. mainly by hand line. This ground is visited principally by small boats, the greater part of the catch being taken by gill nets, although trawls and hand lines also are used here.

The Garden. This is a broken piece of ground lying outside The Elbow and Eagle Island. It runs NNE. and SSW., is about 2 miles long by 1 mile wide, and has depths running from 35 to 60 fathoms. This is a fall ground for hand-line fishing for cod, while haddock, cod, and cusk are found here in the spring. Hake are taken in May and June on the mud about the edges.

Marks: Halfway Rock Light on the big field of Chebeague Island; Eagle Island Woods on the woods in the Eastern Bay.

Sand Shoal. It is ENE. from White Head Grounds 4 miles. This has depths of 18 to 20 fathoms and in species and seasons of their abundance agrees with White Head Ground.

The Elbow. This lies NE. from the Sand Shoal 6 miles from the lightship; S. by E. 4 miles from Halfway Rock. Depths on the shoal parts are 26 fathoms, deepening to 40 fathoms on the edges. The bottom is of rocks and mud. The species and seasons are as on White Head Grounds.

Old Orchard Ground, Wood Island Ground, Cape Porpoise Peaks. Extending over a piece of bottom made up of blue clay with numerous rocky patches, this ground has depths of from 20 to 50 fathoms. Bearing about NE. from Cape Porpoise and distant from 4 to 5 miles, it lies in a N. and S. direction and is about 5 miles long by 1½ miles wide. It is a good spring and summer cod ground, a summer hake ground, and haddock are here in April and May and in the fall and winter and cusk on the deeper parts the year around. This ground is much resorted to by small boats and in winter by some of the larger vessels of the vicinity. Fishing is by hand lines, trawls, and a certain amount by gill netting over the smoother parts.

Marks: The eastern end of Wood Island on the bank at Old Orchard; to the center 6 miles SSE. from Wood Island Light.

Drunken Ledge (Drunkers). Eight miles from Cape Elizabeth; 3 miles N. of Tanta 4 miles S. by E. from the whistling buoy off Cape Elizabeth. Depths are 18 to 40 fathoms on a bottom of sharp rocks. It is about 5 miles long N. and S. by 2 miles wide, extending SSW. and NNE. Cod and cusk are taken the year around; hake in the summer on the mud at edges; haddock from March to June. Fishing is by trawl, hand line, and gill net. Marks: Western Light of Cape Elizabeth on eastern part of woods on Cape until the lightship bears NE.

Eagle Island Ground. This lies S. from Halfway Rock 2 miles. It has a rocky bottom with 20 to 25 fathoms. It is a good cod ground the year around, fished mainly by hand line; there is little trawling here and only a small amount of gill netting.

Flat Ledge; Temple Ledge. Two miles SW. of Bald Head, Cape Small Point, rises a piece of rocky ground from the 20-fathom depths surrounding it. Over the shoal in the center are 5 fathoms, and from this the water deepens on all sides, there being 16 fathoms on the deepest part of the ledge and an average of 20 fathoms about it. The rocky bottom is about 1½ miles long, NE. and SW., by about 3/4 mile wide. The ledge and the hard bottom about it make good gill-netting grounds for cod in the spring months. On the ledge a considerable amount of hand-lining fur cod and pollock is carried on in late May and through June. In the normal seasons of the mackerel fishery this is a good ground on which to seine these fish in June. July, and August. It is also a good lobster ground and is a haddock ground in July and August. Marks: Wallace House in Bald Head Cove on the western edge of Bald Head; Flag Island and the eastern Brown Cow Into line.

The Gully: Mark Island Gully. Bring Seguin over Fullers Rock, 6 miles from Mark Island. This gully lies inside The Elbow. The bottom is sandy on the shoal parts, where there are 50 fathoms; broken and rocky in the deep water in 70 fathoms; and muddy on the edges. It is a good lobster grounds.

Haddock are taken here in the spring months by trawling; cod are taken on trawl and in gill nets during February and March and from Augusta to November. Hake are taken during June, July and August by the sane methods as are used in catching the other species.

New Meadows Channel. West from The Gully; E. from Seguin. This is a spring gill-net ground. Mostly a cod ground.

Pollock Hub. This ground lies SE. from the lightship 6 to 8 miles and 13½ miles S. from Cushings Island bell buoy. It is a rocky piece of bottom, having about 29 fathoms over it. It is about ½ mile across and is fished by hand line, trawl, and gill net, but is mostly a summer hand-line spot. It is a good cod ground in the spring and good for pollock in their season. Between this and Trinidad (SE. by S. from Pollock Hub 3 miles) is a fishing ground for haddock in January and February, on a broken bottom, in depths of from 40 to 60 fathoms. This is both a small-boat and a vessel ground fished by hand line, trawl, and gill nets.

Trinidad. Six miles SE. by S. ½ S. from the lightship off Portland. It is about 2 miles long by 3/4 mile wide, lying in a NNE. and SSW. direction. In general, the bottom is muddy and depths are from 40 to 50 fathoms, except for a shoal about 14 mile across on the northeastern end of the ground, where there is a depth of 32 fathoms over a sharp, rocky bottom.

Haddock are present here in good numbers in February and March. Cod are taken here in gill nets during the summer months, and hake are fairly abundant in the spring over the deeper parts; a few cusk are taken at the same season and in the same depths as the hake are found.

Fire Ground. This ground is E. by S. from the lightship 10 miles. It is a ridge of rocky and gravelly bottom having depths of 35 to 50 fathoms. Its length is 2 miles and its width 1 mile.

Cod and cusk are here the year around, the cod being most abundant in the spring. Haddock are here in February and March: hake are in the deep water on the edges in summer. Fishing here is by hand line, trawl, and gill nets operated by small boats and vessels, the larger craft visiting this ground mostly in the winter, when offshore grounds may not permit of the fishing because of weather conditions. Marks: Bradbury Mountain on Jaquish: Long Reach Mountain (in Quahog Bay) just to westward of Wooded Mark Island, "the length of an oar."

Cod Ledges. These are a succession of rocky patches extending 4½ miles in an ENE. and WSW. direction, with a width of about ½ mile. The southwestern end bears SE. 3/4 S. from Portland Head Light. distant 4 3/4 miles. The northwestern extremity lies 6 or 7 miles ESE. from Portland Head light. The shoalest parts have from 14 to 18 feet of water (Bulwark Shoal: the eastern is Round Shoal). On other parts the depths vary from 5 to 22 fathoms. The bottom is irregular, of rocks and gravel. A favorite small-boat ground for fishermen from Portland and neighboring islands. This is a cod ground the year around and a winter haddock ground.

In June and July a few halibut are taken in 14 to 18 fathoms on the sandy patches between the ledges. We are told "Very many large halibut are sometimes taken in some seasons in this small area. Sid Doughty. a local small-boat fisherman, had $300 worth from half his gear for one day's fishing here, being obliged to leave the rest of his gear until the next day from his weariness in handling the heavy fish alone."

Hue and Cry Bottom. This ground lies W. ½ mile from the Portland Lightship. It is about 2½ miles long by 1½ miles wide and extends in a generally N. and S. direction. The bottom is mainly rocks, though there is a sandy area lying inside it. Depths are from 4 fathoms, where is a buoy and where it breaks in heavy weather, to some 35 fathoms over much of the rest of the ground. Cod and haddock are found here In the spring, and cod, haddock, and cusk in the fall months.

The Pasture. It lies ESE. from the lightship 10 miles: south from The Cow (Small Point) 12 miles. This ground is 4 or 5 miles long by 2½ miles wide. It has depths of from 45 to 80 fathoms over a bottom of broken ground, rocks, and mud. It is a cod ground the year around but is best in spring. Cusk also are here the year around. Haddock usually are plentiful during January, February, and March. Inside the Pasture (about 10 miles S. from The Cow) lies the Fire Ground, mentioned elsewhere.

The Klondike. This ground lies 15 miles S. by E. from Bald Head and is 3 miles long by 2 miles wide. The bottom consists of ridges of rocks—a "blistery" bottom (abundance of "sea pears", "sea squirts", and other marine growths of a similar nature). It is a cod and cusk ground all the year. Haddock are present from January to April and hake from September to December. Depths are from 75 to 80 fathoms over mud and rocks. Fishing on this ground is by hand line and trawl by small boats and sloops, with an occasional trip by larger vessels in winter.

Sagadahoc. This ground is SE. by E. from Halfway Rock 22 miles and S. ½ W. from Seguin 17 miles. It has a broken bottom of rocks "blisters," and mud, and is 3½ miles long by 2½ miles wide, with depths from 50 to 80 fathoms. It is a cusk ground the year around as well as a year-around cod ground, also, but this fishing is at its best in the spring. It is a hake ground on the deeper soundings from September to December. Fishing here is carried on by trawling, hand-lining, and gill netting.

Big Ridge, or Doggetts. These names are given to a piece of fishing ground about 8 miles long by 2 miles wide lying 18 miles SE. by S. ½ S. from the lightship at Portland or 14 miles SE. by E. from the same point, according to which part it is desired to fish upon. It has from 45 on the shoal in the center to 80 fathoms of water on the deeper parts over a bottom of rocks and gravel on the shallower portions and of mud about the edges and in the deeper soundings.

Cod are abundant here in spring and fall on the shoaler parts of the bank and are present the year around on the muddy edges and in the deep water about it; the spring school, however, is the largest. Hake are found in spring and summer on the edges in deep water. A few haddock may be taken in the winter and spring, January to April, inclusive. Cusk can be taken the year around, the best fishing being in spring and winter. The February cusk school is the largest, and the best catches are made in the deep water about the edges of the ground. Fishing here is principally by trawling, but hand-lining and gill netting also are employed, the latter method in continually increasing volume.

Lying off Cape Porpoise, between the bearings of SE. and SSE., and at distances varying from 6 to 8 miles, are a number of small, rocky, or pebbly bottoms having depths ranging from 18 to 25 fathoms. During certain seasons these abound in cod and haddock and are visited by the fishermen of the vicinity.

Tanta. This ground is S. from Cape Elizabeth, the center being distant 12 miles. It is 2 to 3 miles in diameter and has depths of about 40 fathoms over a bottom of broken ground of rocks and gravel. This is a spring and summer fishing ground for cod. Haddock are present here in winter, the best fishing being in January, With a few in the spring. Trawls, hand lines, and gill nets are operated here. Outside of Tanta (S. 3 miles), in 80 and 90 fathoms on muddy and broken bottom (a "punkin" bottom), hake and cusk are abundant in February and March, the hake remaining into the summer. Herring and mackerel usually are present here in those years when their schools arc abundant in this locality.

Winker Ground. The ground lies in a NE. and SW. direction, about 2 miles long by 1/4 mile wide. The bottom is broken, of mud, rocks, and sand, with depths from 35 to 40 fathoms. Outside of the 40-fathom depth the ground is mostly of mud. This is a cod ground in the early spring. haddock and hake being here from July 1 to September 1. Haddock are found here also from March 10 to April 20. This is a small-boat ground, fishing being done mainly by trawling and a certain amount of gill netting. Marks: Run 5 miles SW. from the whistling buoy off Cape Elizabeth. or until Ram Island Winker Light shows out by Cape Elizabeth.

Long Hill Ground. This lies SSE. from Cape Elizabeth, 9 miles to the center. Marks: Bring the western light of Cape Elizabeth on the middle of Johnsons Woods on the high land of the cape, which with the course given before, will bring to the center. This lies in a SSE. and NNW. direction and is a rocky bottom, having 60 to 70 fathoms. Haddock are taken here from October to January 1 and from February 15 to April 1. Cod also occur at about the same season.

Outer and Inner Bumbo. These are two small rocky ridges bearing SE. from The Nubble and extending toward Boon Island. They begin near the main shore and extend nearly to the island. Depths are from 8 to 20 fathoms over a broken piece of bottom, except for a mud gully about 3 miles from the main running NE. and SW. about 3 miles long. In general, this is a small-boat ground, where good catches of cod and haddock are made in spring and fall, especially in the latter season, with good hand-lining for cod in July and August in 8 and 10 fathom depths. These grounds are fished by trawl, hand line and gill nets. All the grounds between Cape Porpoise and Boon Island are good lobster grounds.

Wells Bay. Beside a number of small, rocky patches of fishing ground of less importance, resorted to chiefly by small-boat fishermen and by gill netters from Portsmouth, Wood Island, and Cape Porpoise; this ground has a good cod shoal for spring and winter fishing, which also furnishes good haddocking from April to October. The depths on this are from 25 to 30 fathoms. These are fished by trawl, hand lines, and gill nets (perhaps mainly by the latter) operated by the smaller fishing vessels, chiefly from Portsmouth, Wood island, Cape Porpoise, and Portland.

Lightons. This ground is SE. by E. 8 miles from Cape Porpoise, 3 miles long by 2 miles wide, with depths of 25 to 30 fathoms over a generally gravelly bottom. This is somewhat more productive as a haddock ground from January 1 to March, but cod and hake are numerous in the same season also. A small amount of cod may be taken here in the summer. This is a good lobster ground.

Tracadie; The Acre. This bears NE. by E. from Boon island, distant 5 miles. It is 1 mile in diameter and has a depth of 50 fathoms over a bottom of rocks and gravel. It is a good haddock ground all the year; a cod ground in August, when these fish are "jigged"; a hake ground from April to October; and a cusk ground the year around.

Old Southeast. Extends from the shore soundings at White Island (one of the isles of Shoals) 7 or 8 miles SE. nearly to Jeffreys in a long, rather narrow point. It is a piece of broken ground with a hard bottom, having depths running from 20 fathoms on the inner parts to 50 fathoms farther out and deepening suddenly on all sides to the mud about it. Fish and their seasons are as on Blue Clay, haddock being most abundant on the eastern edge from January through March. This is growing steadily in importance as a gill-netting ground.

The Prairie. This name has been given to a flat ground of generally level bottom, lying E. by N. from Boon Island 7 miles. It has depths of from 41 to 50 fathoms over mud and gravel, rising out of 60 fathoms over the muddy ground about it. It extends in a generally ENE. by WSW. direction, 2 miles long by 1 mile wide. It is a "blistery" ground, the presence of these growths on a rocky or gravelly bottom usually meaning good fishing. This is principally a haddock ground, with the best season from mid March to the 1st of May. This is a small-boat and gill-netting ground. It is also visited to a considerable extent by the larger vessels of the Portland fleet in the severer weather of the winter and early spring because of its accessibility.

Blue Clay Ground. also called Southeast Ground. This bears S. by E. from Boon Island. from which it is distant 8 miles. The form of the ground is roughly square and is from 4 to S miles across. Depths here range from 30 on the shoalest parts to 60 fathoms, the bottom being of tough blue clay. The water deepens suddenly on the muddy ground all about it. It is one of the best winter haddock grounds in this vicinity, particularly the eastern edge, which is much resorted to by haddock trawlers from January through March, when this species is most abundant here. It is a good winter cod ground, also.

A long, narrow strip of hard bottom, separated from the Blue Clay by a narrow mud gully of somewhat greater depth, is called the Prong. Depths here run from 30 fathoms on the inner parts to 70 fathoms offshore. This piece furnishes a very suitable bottom for operating gill nets and is much visited by this type of craft. The Prong lies S. by E. from Cape Porpoise 17 miles. Marks: Bring Acre Hill in line, Notch of Agamenticus at the distance from Cape Porpoise just given. From the Isle of Shoals the Prong is distant 10 miles SE. by E.

Duck Island Ridges. These are two narrow rocky ridges running from Duck Island (one of the Isles of Shoals) toward Boon Island. reaching within I mile of the latter. Depths are from 25 to 30 fathoms. These are good cusk and haddock grounds in the winter and spring, the cusk remaining on the ground also from April to October. This is a cod ground in winter and spring, the fish being taken on the "bobber trawl." which is a trawl of the ordinary type buoyed to "set" 1 fathom or so from the bottom. It is a hand-line ground in summer for cod and pollock. Both small boats and vessels, line trawlers, and gillnetters operate here. It is also a lobster ground.

Boon Island Rock Ground. This ground begins ½ mile eastward of Boon Island Ledge and runs in an ESE. direction 2 or 3 miles from the ledge. It has a bottom of sharp rocks and clay and depths from 40 to 60 fathoms. It is an excellent fishing ground for cod, haddock, and cusk and is one of the best winter fishing grounds for haddock in this vicinity. It is fished mainly by line trawlers but is not much used as yet by gill-netters, being a somewhat difficult piece of bottom for them.

Tower Ground. This is a winter haddock ground having depths averaging 50 fathoms over a ridgy and broken bottom. This is about 3 miles long by 2 miles wide and bears about SE. from Boon Island. Marks: Bring Boon Island Light on the Peak of Mount Agamenticus, running off until the top of the tower and the top of the mountain are level, perhaps 6 miles from Boon Island.

Ten Acre or Nipper Ground. Extends S. ½ E. from Boon Island 6 miles and E. from Isles of Shoals 7 miles. This shoal is about 1/4 mile wide and has 18 to 20 fathoms over clay and mud, the ground sloping gradually to 50 or 60 fathoms near the edge. This is a good fishing ground for cod, haddock, cusk, and pollock in the spring, while on the muddy edges hake are abundant in September. Marks: White Hills over Boon Island on center (these cross bearings meet near the center of the ground); also, the Black Hill W. of Portsmouth over the Star Island of the Isles of Shoals leads to the small rocky shoal that is in the middle of the ground.

Ipswich Bay. This extends from the north side of Cape Ann about to Portsmouth and is resorted to in winter by large schools of cod coming here to spawn. Shore soundings deepen here gradually from the land, reaching 35 to 40 fathoms at 6 or 7 miles out. Within this limit the bottom is mainly sandy, though rocky patches are numerous between Newburyport and Cape Ann. Beyond 40 fathoms the bottom is mainly mud.

The principal cod-fishing grounds of Ipswich Bay lie off the northern shore, from Newburyport to the entrance of Portsmouth Harbor, 1½ to 5 miles off the land In 12 to 25 fathoms. Cod are taken abundantly off Boars Head, also. During 1923 and 1924 the cod fishing in these waters, especially off Boars Head, was the best for some years. Fishing is done by trawls and hand-lining, and of late years a large and increasing gill-netting fleet has operated in these waters, especially from March to June.

The muddy ground outside these waters Is a hake ground much frequented by small boats and vessels from the Isles of Shoals and Cape Ann during the summer and fall. "Flounder dragging" Is a considerable industry in these waters, the craft employed being a small type of the otter trawler, mainly operating out of Newburyport on a piece of shallow mud bottom extending from NE. by E. to SE. of the Isles of Shoals and on another ESE. from Thacher Island. Depths are from 4 to 14 fathoms.

Massachusetts Bay. The larger part of this ground, especially inside Stellwagens Bank, has a mud bottom, on which large quantities of fish are rarely taken. On the shore soundings between Boston Harbor and Plymouth to Sandwich are many rocky ledges, which are favorite feeding grounds for cod In winter and fall. Off Plymouth, in late March, there is generally a large school of codfish, from which the gill-netters take good fares. All over this ground in depths of from 10 to 40 fathoms. netters from Gloucester and Boston operate in a codfishery In the months of December, January, and February. There is a considerable hand-line fishery for pollock in the fall. The gill-netters also take large fares of this species on these shore grounds as well as about Gloucester, their fares for a single month often amounting to nearly 4,000,000 pounds. November and December usually show the largest catches. These vessels operate mostly between Boston and Gloucester, and their catch goes principally to "the splitters." since the abundance of the fish naturally operates to reduce its price. This pollock netting comes to an abrupt end with the closing days of January, when the fish move offshore.

Herring appear about Cape Ann in September in large numbers in most years, the fishing lasting about two weeks, when the school moves slowly inward toward the head, and the last catches usually are taken off Minot Light, Boston. The mackerel, after leaving the coast of Maine in their autumnal migrations, pass by Cape Ann and enter Massachusetts Bay during October and November, where they are taken in great number by purse seiners, netters, and pound nets, of which latter there are many in Cape Cod Bay, and which take many mackerel and herring in their seasons.

Near the center of Cape Cod Bay, on a line between Race Point and Cape Cod Canal, lies a rocky elevation on which cod are taken, known as Eagle Ledge or Bay Ledge, and by Provincetown fishermen as Red Bank. It has a depth of 13 fathoms. Cape Cod Bay has a considerable Industry in flounder dragging, the fish being taken by a small type of otter trawl. South and southeast of Thacher Island from 5 to 8 miles lies a stretch of muddy bottom with patches of sand scattered over it, where a considerable amount of this method of fishing is carried on during most of the year.

Old Man's Pasture. This ground is due S. from Thacher Island, SE. from Eastern Point Light. Cape Ann, and distant 5 miles. It is about 3/4 mile long, NNE. and SSW. by 1/ mile wide. The bottom is rough and rocky, with about 24 fathoms average depths. It is a cod ground for the entire year, which fish are taken by gill-netters principally in November. Pollock are taken here, also by gill-netters, from October 1 to December. Apparently there are few haddock here in the fall, but there is good fishing for these from February to April 1. It is also a lobster ground.

Harts Ground. This lies S. 1/4 E. from Eastern Point Light. distant 5½ miles. It is 3/4 mile long in an ENE. and WSW. direction by 1/4 mile wide, and is a small, rocky patch with a depth of 30 fathoms. It is a summer haddock ground, visited mainly by small boats. There is little or no gill netting here.

Eagle Ridge, sometimes called Little Middle Bank. This ridge is 7 2/3 miles S. by W. from Eastern Point Light, Cape Ann. and 1 mile long, NE. and SW., by ½ mile wide. The average depths are 25 fathoms on a rocky and uneven bottom. Formerly, with Old Man's Pasture and Browns Ledge. this was considered the principal winter grounds of the cod, but not so many have been taken here at that season in recent years.

Inside this area, at an average distance of 2½ miles from Eastern Point Light and between bearings S. ½ E. and SW.. are a number of small, rocky patches having depths of from 10 to 25 fathoms—Browns Ledge, Spot of Rocks, Saturday Night Ledge, and Burnhams Rocks; SW ½ W. from Saturday Night Ledge, 6 miles, lies Old Tillie. Farther in are two shoal spots bearing nearly west from Eastern Point. one at 3/4 mile and the other at 2 miles distance, each having 11 fathoms. The first is called Eleven Fathom Ground. the second, Kettle Island Ledge. This latter lies ½ mile SE. of Kettle Island. These are cod grounds in winter and haddock grounds in summer. Gill-netters operate from Kettle Island to Halfway Rock and Italian boats trawl at all seasons off The Graves.

Western Point Ridge. This bears S. by E. ½ E. from Eastern Point Light, distant 9 1/4 miles. Its length NE. and SW. is 1½ miles and its width is ¾ mile. The depths average 29 fathoms over a broken and rocky bottom. Small vessels and boats fish here for cod and haddock in the summer. Netters take many pollock on all these shore grounds in the fall runs, October to January furnishing the largest fares. Apparently these are spawning fish that leave abruptly during January, working offshore again.

The Dump. This lies inside the lightship at Boston, extending from this to and well into Nahant Bay. On these inner grounds soundings are from 12 to 15 fathoms over sand and gravel. This portion is a cod ground from March to May. The outer parts of the ground have from 15 to 20 fathoms of water over a gravelly and muddy bottom, which usually furnishes haddocking during the early spring. These are mainly gill-net grounds.

Inner Bank. This lies SE. from Thacher Island 12 miles to the northern end, whence it extends in a generally southerly direction for about 10 miles, having an average width of 2½ miles. Depths here average about 40 fathoms on a hard, gravelly bottom, where haddock usually are taken in the spring, pollock in the fall, and cod in the winter months. This piece of ground is much fished by the gill-netting fleet out of Gloucester.

A large area of muddy ground lying E. of this and between it and Middle Bank is much visited by the flounder draggers out of Boston and Gloucester. Depths here are from 40 to 55 fathoms over a comparatively smooth bottom.

A ridge that lies just S. of the Limiter Bank, and which may be a continuation of it, extends from a point E. by N. from Scituate buoy to a point SE. by S. from the same about 10 or 11 miles and furnishes cod fishing in February, beginning at Brewers Spot, on the southern end of the ground, and working northward with the schools to Si's Spot, at the northern end of the ridge. The bottom over much of the ridge is of mussel beds, with from 25 to 30 fathoms of water, but at the northern end it is rocky and pebbly, with from 30 to 35 fathoms and on the southern end the bottom is composed of stones, gravel, and pebbles with 20 to 25 fathoms of water over it. This ridge is flanked E. and W. by a muddy bottom, which furnishes the flounder-dragging fleet with good fishing during most of the year.

Table 2—Inner Fishing Grounds, showing the principal species taken upon them.

Fishing ground	Cod	Haddock	Hake	Pollock	Cusk	Halibut	Herring	Mackerel	Lobsters	Miscellaneous
Great Ledge	x	x		x		x			x	
Barnum Head Ground	x	x	x	x						
Peterson Ground	x		x							
Cusk Ridge	x		x		x					
Potato Patch	x		x		x					
The Apron	x	x		x	x					
Henry Gallants Ridge	x				x					
Middle Ground; Mosers	x	x					x	x	x	
Johns Head Ground	x									
White Island Ground	x	x					x			
Steamboat Ground	x	x	x	x	x				x	
Inner and Outer Boutens	x	x	x		x				x	
Hill Ground	x		x	x					x	
Seguin Sou' Sou' West	x								x	
Seguin Ridge	x	x	x	x	x					
Seguin Ground	x	x	x	x					x	
McIntire Reef	x		x						x	
Seguin Hub	x	x	x	x					x	
Cow Ground	x				x				x	
Murre Hub	x	x	x							
Mistaken Ground	x	x	x	x	x					
Tag Ground	x	x	x	x	x					
Kettle Bottom, Outer	x	x			x					
Murray Hole	x		x							
Inner Kettle	x	x			x					
Bantam	x	x	x							
White Head Ground	x	x	x		x	x				
Green Ground	x									
Lambo	x	x	x							
The Bull Ground	x	x	x							
The Garden	x	x	x		x					
Sand Shoal	x	x	x		x	x				
The Elbow	x	x	x		x					
Old Orchard; Wood Island Ground	x	x	x		x					
Drunken Ledge	x	x	x		x					
Eagle Island Ground	x									
Flat Ledge; Temple Ledge	x	x		x				x	x	
The Gully	x	x	x						x	
New Meadows Channel	x									
Pollock Hub	x	x		x						
Trinidad	x	x	x		x					
Fire Ground	x	x	x		x					
Cod Ledges	x	x				x			x	
Hue and Cry	x	x			x					
The Pasture	x	x			x					
The Klondike	x	x	x		x					
Sagadahoc	x		x		x					
Doggetts; Big Ridge	x	x	x		x			x	x	
Tanta	x	x	x		x		x	x		
The Winker Ground	x	x	x							
Long Hill Ground	x	x								
Little Hill Ground	x	x		x	x					
Humbo, Outer and Inner	x	x							x	
Wells Bay	x	x								
Lightons	x	x		x					x	
Tracadie	x	x		x	x					
Old Southeast	x	x								
The Prairie		x								
Blue Clay, Southeast	x	x							x	
Duck Island Ridges	x	x			x	x			x	
Boon Island Rock Ground	x	x				x				
Tower Ground		x								
Ten Acres; Nipper Ground	x	x		x	x	x				
Ipswich Bay	x		x							x
Massachusetts Bay	x		x		x		x	x		x
Old Man's Pasture	x	x			x				x	
Harts Ground		x								
Eagle Ridge	x	x								
Western Point Ridge	x	x		x						
The Dump	x	x								
Inner Bank	x	x			x					
Brewers and Si's Spot	x									x

¹ Flounder.

OUTER GROUNDS

Grand Manan Bank. This bank is at the entrance of the Bay of Fundy, SW. ½ S. from the southwest head of Grand Manan Island from which the northern part of the bank is 15 miles distant. From Mount Desert Rock, E. by S., it is 45 miles distant. The bank is 10 miles long and 5 miles wide, extending in a NE. and SW. direction. The bottom is mostly stones and gravel, the depths running from 24 to 45 fathoms. Soundings of 18 and 21 fathoms are found on the northeast part.

Cod (especially abundant when the June school is on the ground) and pollock are the principal fish. Haddock are not usually abundant, although sometimes they are plentiful in the fall from late September to December; hake are fairly abundant on the mud between Grand Manan Bank and the Middle Ground (In The Gully). This is a good halibut bank, the fish being in 33 to 60 fathoms in June and July; the southwest soundings and the southeast soundings are most productive always. The best fishing season is from April to October, when the fish come to this bank to feed. In the spring the fish, other than halibut, are mostly on the southwest part, but later (July to October) the best fishing is had on the northern edge of the ground. The very best herring fishing for large herring (food fish) occurs on this bank in June and July. In general, this is a small-vessel ground fished by craft from Cutler, Eastport, Grand Manan, and, to a less extent, Yarmouth, Nova Scotia, with an occasional visit by craft from Portland and Rockland, chiefly trawlers of moderate size.

Tides run NE. in flood and SW. on the ebb and are quite strong, the flood being the heaviest. Because of these powerful currents, fishing is somewhat difficult, it being necessary to make sets at the slack of the tides, getting the gear over and traveling with the finish of the current, to take it up and come back with the tide's return.

Middle Ground. This ground is between Grand Manan Bank and Marblehead Bank; its length from NW. to SE. is 1½ miles, and it is about ½ mile wide. Depths averaging 37 fathoms are found on the southern edge on a hard, rocky bottom, increasing to over 60 fathoms over much of the ground. The remainder of the bank has a bottom of sand and gravel. There is a shoal of 28 fathoms near the center with a bottom of rocks and stones. The species and seasons of their abundance are much as on Grand Manan

Bank and German Bank, but the Middle Ground is rather better as a cod ground than as a ground for other species, June, perhaps, being the best month for the fishing.

Marblehead Bank. Situated between Grand Manan and German Banks, the shoal water bearing SSE. from Moosabec Light, distant 32 miles. It is from 12 to 15 miles long and 7 or 8 miles wide, lying between 44° 00′ and 44° 10′ north latitude and 66° 58′ and 67° 13′ west longitude. There are from 35 to 70 fathoms of water over it; the bottom is mostly clay and gravel. The principal fishing is for cod, pollock, and haddock, but there are more or less hake and cusk to be had from this ground.

The best fishing season is from early spring through the early part of the summer, and this ground is of little account after July. The same type of vessels operate here as on the neighboring banks, with an occasional larger vessel. The craft are mostly hand-liners from Cutler, Jonesport, and Rockland, with a few vessels from the trawl fleets of Portland and others from the Canadian Provinces. Haddock are found in the shoal water from May to October. Cusk are on the eastern portion in from 60 to 70 fathoms virtually the year around. Many large hake are present on the western edge in 80 to 90 fathoms in the summer. The June and July cod school is the best, but this species is present in smaller numbers all the year. Halibut are found all over the bank, being especially abundant in the eastern shoal water in spring and summer (April to October). It seems necessary to leave the halibut trawls down for a longer set here than on other grounds in order to make a good catch.

German Bank. This is one of the most important banks in the Bay of Fundy. (We are here referring to the German Bank in the bay and not to the part of Seal Island ground, so marked on some charts.) It bears SE. from Bakers Island Light, Mount Desert, from which the northeast part is about 52 miles distant. Its length is about 15 miles, the width 9 or 10 miles. It lies between 43° 38′ and 43° 53′ north latitude and 64° 58′ and 67° 15′ west longitude. Depths are from 65 to 100 fathoms with soundings of 47 fathoms on the northern part. The bottom is mostly tough red clay with spots of mud, sand, gravel, and pebbles on some parts. The tides set in and out over this bank to and from the Bay of Fundy, the ebb SW. and the flood NE., but the currents are not so strong as might be expected.

Cod, hake, and cusk are the principal species taken, with pollock and haddock in lesser amounts. It is a fairly good halibut ground also, wherever a bottom of black and white gravel is found, though formerly little regarded as such. The fish (except hake) are most abundant in the spring. This ground is not much fished of late years, but was formerly considered a good place for hake fishermen in summer. Probably it is equally as good now, but the demand for hake has diminished materially in recent years, and this fishery has suffered in consequence. Mostly Maine vessels fish this bank, from Cutler, Moosabec, and Rockland, with a few from Portland and perhaps an occasional visitor from the Yarmouth, Nova Scotia, fleet.

Newfound. This ground is 45 miles SE. by S. from Mount Desert Rock and has depths of 90 to 100 fathoms over a gravelly bottom. It is about 12 to 15 miles long. ENE. and WSW., by 7 miles wide, lying in the track of the Yarmouth (Nova Scotia) to Boston steamers. Apparently, this title is given to some rediscovered old ground and with a new generation of fishermen displaces the old name. This is not a haddock ground, but cod, cusk, and hake (large fish) are abundant here in the spring. Perhaps this is an all-the-year fishing ground, but thus far no further information about it has been obtainable. It is about 12 to 15 miles long, ENE aned WSW, by 7 miles wide, lying in the track of the Yarmouth (Nova Scotia) to Boston steamers.

Jones Ground. This is an important cod ground though of small size. The western part bears SE, from Bakers Island Light, distant 32 miles. The ground is 10 to 12 miles long, NE. and SW. and 5 miles wide. Depths range from 50 to 100 fathoms. The bottom, which is quite broken, consists of rocks, gravel, and mud. On the northeast parts, where depths vary from 50 to 70 fathoms, the bottom is rocky and rough. This part bears SE. by E. ½ E. from Bakers Island Light, distant 35 miles. (Green Mountain, of Mount Desert, bears NW.) It is a hake ground in 110 fathoms. The center of the ground furnishes good trawl fishing from May 1 to September. The principal catch is large cod, but a smaller amount of hake, cusk, and pollock are taken also.

Bank Comfort. This is a comparatively little known fishing ground lying SE. by S. from Mount Desert Rock. distant 12 or 13 miles. It is said to be 5 miles long, SW. and NE., by 3 miles wide. Here are depths of from 75 to 80 fathoms over a hard gravelly bottom, the shoalest water being some 65 fathoms. This is an excellent ground but little fished because its small size makes it somewhat difficult to find. It is a very good cod ground in spring and summer, hand-liners catching large cod here from May to August. Hake and cusk are present here in summer also. It is scarcely fished at any other than the seasons mentioned.

Clay Bank. This bank lies SW. by W. from Mount Desert Rock, the center distant 7 miles. It is 4 miles long, WSW. and ENE., by 2 miles wide. Depths are from 50 to 80 fathoms over a bottom of hard clay. Cod are the principal catch in spring, hake in summer. There is virtually no winter fishing.

Newfound. This ground lies off of the northeast edge of Jeffreys Bank and is often considered a part of it, but there seems to lie deep water between.

This is one of three grounds of the name in these waters. The present piece of bottom lies 20 miles SE. by S. from Matinicus block and S. ½ E. from Seal Island (in Penobscot Bay) and has a broken and irregular bottom with depths from 60 to 100 fathoms over blue mud and shells and considerable areas of gravelly ground. It is about 7 miles long, E. by N. and W. by S., and about 4 miles wide.

Fishing here in the summer months is mostly by hand-lining because of the presence of schools of dogfish in these waters at that season. In the spring it is a good ground for cod, and in the fall months cod, hake, and cusk are taken, all by trawling. Perhaps March is the best month for cod fishing here, the cusk being most numerous at the same season, when they are especially abundant in depths of 80 fathoms or more and are then taken by trawling. In spring and early summer halibut are often found in depths of 35 to 60 fathoms on the gravelly parts of the ground.

A small rocky eminence just off the northern edge of the ground rises sharply from the 94-fathom depths surrounding it to reach 48 fathoms. On this are taken market cod (2½ to 10 pounds weight) during the spring months and very large cod (fish reaching 50, 60, and 70 pounds or more) during June, July, and August. Its small area makes this spot somewhat difficult to find.

Jeffreys Bank. This ground lies east of Cashes Bank and, despite its considerable size, is of comparatively little importance as a fishing ground. It is about 20 miles long. SW. and NE., and 10 miles wide. The northern and southern limits are 43° 30' and 43° 15' north latitude. The eastern edge is In 68° 25', the western in 68° 45'. west longitude. The bottom is somewhat broken—mud, sand, gravel, and pebbles, with a great number of small rocky ridges, upon which good fishing is generally to be had, although these spots are quite difficult to find and accommodate but little trawl gear. There is virtually no fishing upon much of the interior parts of the bank between these spots, where the bottom is mostly of mud. Depths over the bank vary from 35 to 70 fathoms. The Outer Fall and the Inner Fall. generally called Monhegan Fall, are the only parts of Jeffreys Bank thought to be of much importance as fishing grounds. Both these formerly furnished excellent fishing but are not now as much resorted to, although vessels from Portland and Rockland often fish here and bring in fair catches.

Cod, haddock, and cusk are the most important species in the fares from this ground, with a lesser amount of pollock and a few halibut, these latter usually being taken on the small ridges above mentioned In the main, this bank is a winter ground; good also in the spring and early summer before the dogfish strike it. It is fished mostly by the smaller vessels—trawlers of from 15 to 70 tons.

The Inner Fall lies SE. ½ S. from Monhegan Island, 21½ miles, west of Newfound 6 miles, and S. by W ½ W. from Matinicus Rock 17 miles. The Outer Fall lies S. ½ E. from Matinicus Rock 21 miles. These both have hard sharp bottoms, which are good cod and cusk grounds in the spring. The gravelly bottom, both on the Inner Fall and on the Outer Fall, often holds halibut in the spring and early summer (May 1 to July 15) in depths of from 35 to 60 fathoms. The fishing ground of the Inner Fall is somewhat difficult to find, the best portions lying in a narrow strip about 6 miles long by something less than 1 mile wide along the northwestern edge of the bank.

Soundings ranging from 35 to 55 fathoms over the main body of the bank drop suddenly to 85 and even 94 on the edges. The average depth is about 45 fathoms over a rocky bottom, with good cod fishing in summer and cusk on the hard bottom of the deeper water. Haddock usually are abundant on this bank in winter. Along the northern edge of Jeffreys Bank, between the Inner Fall and the Outer Fall, in an average depth of 40 fathoms, cod and halibut are taken in spring and summer. The extreme southern part of the bank is also a fairly good cod ground, while halibut occur in fair numbers in summer. Depths here are from 38 to 45 fathoms over rocks and gravel.

A small circular piece of ground rises about 2 miles W. of the bank, lying between it and Toothaker Ridge. This is about 2 miles across and has depths averaging 50 fathoms over a rocky bottom. This spot is a good summer cod ground.

Toothaker Ridge. This bank is 26 miles S. ½ E. from Monhegan and lies in an ENE. and WSW. direction. There seem to be two ridges here, the larger being about 5 or 6 miles long by about 1½ miles wide. This inner ridge has a shoal of 35 fathoms on the western end, from which it deepens eastward to about 45 fathoms, which is the general depth elsewhere on this piece of ground.

The outer ridge parallels the inner at about 1½ miles distance and there is a deep, narrow gully between. It apparently has about half the area of the other. This smaller ridge has a 45-fathom shoal of rocks on the western end, deepening the water, like the other, to the eastward to 75 and 80 fathoms over a broken rocky bottom and 90 fathoms on hard mud. This is an all-the-year cusk ground. A few cod are present all the year. but this species is most abundant here and on the other ridge in the spring and through June. Hake occur on the muddy ground in summer and fall.

On both shoals are abundant growths of "lemons" and like species of fish food, and they are good "hand-line spots" over their rocky bottoms.

Fishing on both is said to be at its best in the spring and in June, the species taken being cod, cusk, pollock, and hake. As before stated, these are year-around cod and cusk ground, pollock and hake being present in summer and fall, the latter species over the muddy ground. These grounds have been thought to lie too rough for trawling. But occasional good fares are taken on them by this method.

Cashes Bank. Our older reports state that Cashes Bank was not then an important fishing ground except for a short time in the spring, although good fares were often taken there in the fall also. The writer has found it furnishing at least its quota in recent years and in apparently increasing volume. It bears E. 1/4 S. from Cape Ann (Thacher Island Light, from which point most skippers lay their course), from which its shoaler parts are distant 78 miles, and bears SE. 1/4 S. from Portland Lightship 69 miles to the buoy upon it, where is a depth of 17 fathoms; and 74 miles SE. ½ S. from Cape Elizabeth eastern light to the buoy. The bank is about 22 miles long, from 42° 49′ to 43° 11′ north latitude, and about 17 miles wide, from 68° 40′ to 69° 03′ west longitude. There are three small shoals upon its western part, of which the southern has a depth of 7 fathoms, the middle one has 4 fathoms, and the northern one has 11 fathoms. The middle shoal lies in 42° 56′ north latitude and 68° 52′ west longitude. From this the south shoal bears S. by E. and the north shoal NNE., each being 3 1/4 miles distant from it. The water breaks on these in rough weather and, though of small extent, they are dangerous to passing vessels bound from Cape Sable to Massachusetts ports, across whose course they lie directly. Except for these shoals, the water ranges from 15 to 60 fathoms. The ground is more or less broken, and the bottom is of sand, pebbles, and rocks.

The principal fishing on these grounds is for cod, haddock, hake, and cusk; the cod and cusk are present the year around, the cod being most abundant in February, March. and April in an average depth of 60 fathoms. The hake are found on the muddy edges in summer, with a lesser number present all the year. Haddock are present in considerable numbers from November to February, and sometimes a good school occurs in 20-fathom depths in April. The arrival of the dogfish usually puts a temporary ending to the fishing here in the last days of June or early In July, to be resumed again when these pests have moved inshore. Formerly halibut were reported as seen rarely, but of late years they have been found among the kelp in 15 to 18 fathoms on the shoal nearly the year around, the fish ranging in size from 5 to 40 pounds, rarely larger. Halibut of larger size are taken occasionally in fairly good numbers in 30 to 50 fathoms in May and June. Perhaps this species is more abundant on this and neighboring grounds than is generally realized. At all events, certain Portland vessels have recently taken good fares of halibut when fishing for them here in the season named. Cusk are present in the deep water the year around. As is the case with most of the detached ridges in this gulf, the cusk is the most abundant of the fish present about the middle of March. continuing in good numbers through May. In herring years these fish usually occur in good numbers on this ground In late May, and a considerable number of these (food fish or large herring) are taken here by seiners at this season. Mackerel are generally abundant on these grounds In those years when these fish occur In normal quantities on this coast.

Vessels operating on Cashes Bank range in size from 15 to 50 tons, principally from Maine ports, with a fair number of them from Gloucester and Boston, especially in winter. Of late years a few gill-netters have fished here, and these craft are using these grounds in steadily increasing numbers.

A comparatively little known and apparently as yet unnamed ridge lies E. by S. 15 miles from the buoy on Cashes Ledge, which is reported to be good fishing ground, especially for cod and cusk. With both species present here the year around, the cod is said to be most abundant in April and May: and the cusk, as is the rule on these outlying ridges, appears in largest numbers in March and April. Haddock seem to be somewhat rare here.

This ridge lies in a SE. and NW. direction, extending somewhat indefinitely but for at least 10 miles by about 3 miles in width. On the ridge the bottom is broken—a hard bottom of black gravel, which usually means a good fishing spot—the depths here being from 85 to 90 fathoms. There are numerous muddy spots between these harder pieces of ground where soundings run to 100 fathoms or slightly more. The surrounding bottom is mostly of mud, and the depths average from 100 to 125 fathoms. There are a number of pieces of gravelly hard ground in the vicinity, each of which probably would furnish equally good fishing for cod and cusk at the same seasons as on the ridge.

Due E. from the buoy on Ammens Rock about 12 miles lies a ridge that rises from the 100 to 120 fathom depths about it to a depth of about 80 fathoms over a bottom of broken ground, mud, and shells. This shoaler piece is some 3 miles long. N. by E. and S. by NW., by 1 mile wide. It furnishes good fishing for cod, hake, and cusk in the spring, April being the best season.

A ridge lying NW. of Cashes Bank and nearly parallel with the main bank, only separated by a narrow deep channel, is about 7 miles long by 1½ miles wide. The species and the seasons are the same here as on Cashes Bank.

Big Ridge (near Cashes Bank). This is a broken and rocky piece of bottom running from the tip of the southeastern part of the ground, at about 10 miles S. from the buoy on Ammens Rock and about 82 miles SE. ½ S. from the lightship at Portland, to a point about 20 miles S. by E. from the buoy named. Its length is not to be stated definitely, and it is probably greater than here shown. The width averages about 1½ to 2 miles. Depths are from 65 to 80 fathoms and more, increasing gradually as it goes away from the main bank. The species and their seasons of abundance here are as on Cashes Bank. Perhaps this is more of a cod and cusk ground than is the main part of Cashes Bank, the cusk being particularly abundant during March and April. Halibut also are found here in May and June in from 50 to 60 fathoms of water. A considerable amount of the fish shown in the table of the catch from the area included in Cashes Bank may very well have come from this piece of ground.

Another big ridge, paralleling the 100-fathom curve of Georges Bank at about 20 miles N. of it, lies SE by S from the buoy on Cashes Ledge, forty miles to its center; SE by S 110 miles from Portland Lightship; ESE 92 miles from Cape Ann to its western end, and E. by S. ½ S. from the ship at Boston 100 miles. This ridge also is of somewhat indefinite area, being perhaps 20 miles long in an ESE by WNW direction by 1½ to three miles wide. Apparently depths are fairly uniform from 85 to 95 fathoms, the bottom of the ridge being of coarse black sand and having blue mud in the deeper area around it. This is said to be a good cod and cusk ground the year round.

John Dyers Ridge. This lies 14 miles S. by E. from Toothakers Ridge, 40 miles S. by E. from Monhegan Island, and 7 miles NE. from Cashes Bank. It is about 5 miles long by 2 miles wide, lying in an ENE. and WSW. direction. The water is shoalest on the western edge, where are from 45 to 50 fathoms over a sharp, pebbly bottom; thence the ground slopes to the NE. into 75 and 80 fathoms over a hard, gravelly, and muddy bottom, in all other directions falling off sharply to 90 and 100 fathom soundings over a muddy bottom.

This is essentially a cod ground for the entire year, the species being most abundant from May 1 to November. It is a cusk ground all the year on the hard bottom of the deeper parts, March and April showing the largest schools. Hake also are abundant in 70 fathoms and deeper on the mud in summer and fall.

Fifty-five Fathom Bunch. West of Cashes Bank is a rocky ridge extending ENE. and WSW. about 4 miles and having a width of about 1 mile. This is mainly a cod ground, the seasons for the species being as on Cashes Bank.

Fippenies Bank. This consists of two shoals averaging 80 fathoms in depth with a channel of 90 fathoms between them. These run NE. and SW., the eastern shoal about 8 miles long by 1 mile wide, the western about half as large. Fippenies bears E. 1/4 S. from Thacher Island, distant 61 miles; from Portland Lightship, SE. by S. ½ S, 57 miles to the western point of the northern shoal in 35 fathoms. The bank is nearly 10 miles long NE. and SW. and averages 4½ miles wide. The bottom is of gravel, pebbles, and clay, having depths over much of the shoal of about 30 fathoms but also from 36 to 60 fathoms. It is fished by the shore fleet in the spring and early summer. The fish and seasons are as on Cashes Bank. Formerly twice as many haddock were taken here as on Cashes or on Platts Bank, but this has changed in recent years. Halibut are taken here in fair numbers in 45 to 55 fathom depths in June, July, and August on the "black gravel" of the southern and western edge. The "white gravel" on the north shoal is of little account as a fishing ground, since it is composed mostly of the shells of dead scallops.

The Ridge (on the southern part of Fippenies). This is SSE. from the light-ship at Portland 75 miles and has a bottom of yellow mud and pebbles and depths of 75 to 95 fathoms. Cod are present here in December and January; cusk the year around, but most numerous in February and March; haddock in December and January; hake in September and October. The length of this bank is from 4 to 5 miles and the width somewhat less than 2 miles. It lies in an ENE. and WSW. direction.

Maurice Lubee's Ground. This lies outside of New Ledge (Platts Bank) 47 miles SSE. from the lightship at Portland. Extending in an ENE. and WSW. direction, its boundaries are somewhat indefinite. It is perhaps 8 miles long by 3 miles wide and has depths from 95 to 110 fathoms over a bottom consisting mostly of mud.

Cusk are plentiful here in the spring, with a few in the fall. Cod are taken all the year around, the Spring school being the largest. Hake are most numerous In the spring and fall months, and haddock are not common but are most numerous in winter.

Apparently the abundance of cod on this ground is due to the great quantity of shrimps and soft-shelled crabs found on the muddy bottom and on the rocks that compose this ground. There seem to be many of these deep-water grounds between and about the shoaler grounds, as near Cashes, Fippenies, and Jeffreys, which apparently serve as fairways over which the schools of hake, cod, and cusk, move from Georges Bank into the Gulf of Maine in the spring of the year.

Harvey Blacks Ridge. This is SE. ½ S. from the lightship off Portland, distant 42 miles, and SE. from New Ledge, distant 8 miles. From Glovers Rock, off Small Point, Me. this ridge lies SE. by S. ½ S. 41 miles. It extends in an ENE. and WSW. direction about 4 miles long by I mile wide. Depths average 70 to 100 fathoms over a bottom of yellow clay and gravel. Cod are taken here all the year. Haddock are found in the deep water in the spring: cusk all the year in deep water, together with hake in summer, also on the muddy bottom in deep water. Pollock and other surface-schooling fish are found here in their proper season.

The Cod Ridge (formerly Outer Harris Ground). This lies NE. from the Northeast Peak of New Ledge, distant 7 miles. It extends in an ENE. and WSW. direction, the ground narrowing and the water deepening to the eastward, the shoal ground having 45 fathoms on a bottom of small pebbles and fine black gravel and sand, depths increasing in all other directions to 100 fathoms on the mud and sloping off somewhat steeply, especially on the southeast side, where the drop is very sharp. The length of the ground is about 5 miles, the width 1 mile. This is an all-the-year cod ground, the season of greatest abundance being from May 1 to November. The haddock are usually In their greatest numbers here from January 1 to April. Apparently no large number of cusk or hake are taken here on the ridge, perhaps because the water is not deep enough for the former, except for the small fish, which are of little value to the fishermen; and the ground is not muddy enough for the latter species. Both species, however, are found about the edges in the deep water, the cusk on the sharpest, hardest part of the bottom (perhaps most common in February and March), the hake, as usual, on the muddy parts about it.

Three-Dory Ridge. Outside of New Ledge and about midway between it and Harvey Blacks Ridge is a small ridge about 3 miles long, running NE. and SW., and about ½ mile wide. This lies SE. by S. from the Portland Lightship. 38 miles to the shoal of 55 fathoms, which is near its center. From this the ground slopes away on all sides to 63 and 65 fathom depths over which area the bottom is made up of sand, gravel, mud, and rocks. At these lower depths are found "pipes" (clay cylinders), where the fishing ends abruptly. All about the ridge are depths of 80 to 100 fathoms on a bottom of mud. This is almost entirely a cod ground, good from May to August.

Platt's Bank or New Ledge. This bears E. by N. ½ N. from Thacher Island, from which the shoal portion of the ledge is distant 53 miles. From Portland Lightship it is 30 miles SSE. to the center of the ground. The bank is about 12 miles long, NE. and SW.. and about 8 miles wide. The western shoal, which is of small extent and rocky and which has a considerable amount of dead shells upon it, is situated near the center, its depth being 29 fathoms. From this shoal to the Southwest Peak is about 11 miles SW. by S. Another shoal lies E. 3 miles, having about 30 fathoms over sand and gravel, which is a good fall ground for haddock. East-northeast from the western shoal 3 miles brings us to a rocky ridge, with spots of hard mud and pebbles between, in 65-fathom depth, which is a fine winter cusk ground, these fish remaining here until April. Over much of the bank the depths range from 30 to 35 fathoms with a bottom of rocks and gravel. From the edge of the shoaler area the bottom slopes gradually to 50 or 60 fathoms, beyond which it drops suddenly to 80 or 90 fathoms over a muddy bottom.

This was considered one of the very best fishing grounds for cod and haddock in the Gulf of Maine, but the haddock catch here has fallen off recently. Hake also are very abundant during the summer months and often during October on the muddy bottom near the edge. Inside 100 fathoms, on a "punkin" bottom of rocks and gravel, near the mud, haddock are found from December to March. Cod, pollock, and cusk occur from May to October, the former on the rocky and gravelly portions, the latter on the deep soundings, with the Northeast Peak the best summer ground. This is also an especially good fall and winter ground for haddock. Halibut are often found in 35 fathoms (small fish) from September through November; also In spring and early summer. This ground is fished by vessels from Cape Cod, Mass., to Cutler, Me., mainly by trawling, some hand-lining, but no gill netting of importance as yet.

Jeffreys Ledge. Jeffreys Ledge may be considered one of the best fishing grounds in the Gulf of Maine, although of comparatively small size. It appears to be an extension of the shoal ground that makes off in an easterly direction from Cape Ann, it is about 20 miles long in a NE. and SW. direction and about 4 miles wide. Its southern limits is 42° 54′ and its northern limit 43° north latitude; its eastern and western boundaries may be placed at 69° 58′ and 70° 18′ west longitude. The bottom is rocky on the shoaler parts, with gravel and pebbles on the edges. Depths on the bank are from 27 to 35 fathoms, falling off to 40 or 50 on the edges. The shoalest water lies from 4 to 5 miles N. by E. from the buoy, where there is 22 fathoms. Ordinarily there is little or no tide, with an occasional current SW. There are, however, strong westerly currents with the heavy easterly winds, and often after a period of mild weather with no strong tides there will suddenly develop a heavy SW. flow, indicating the approach of a strong northwester. This seems a general rule in the Gulf of Maine and is, perhaps, prevalent over much of our North Atlantic coast.

Jeffreys Ledge bears S. ½ W. from the lightship off Portland, 19 miles to the northern edge and 22 miles S. from the buoy on the Hue and Cry to the edge of the shoal.

A small cove makes for a short distance into the western side of Jeffreys Ledge at about 20 miles from Boon Island in a SE. by S. ½ S. direction. The bottom in the cove is broken and muddy, with depths of about 60 fathoms. Thence, the ground slopes away to the mouth, where the edges about the entrance are rocky and have 70 and 75 fathom depths. These rocky areas are cusk grounds in January, February, and March, during which months the cove itself usually furnishes good haddock fishing. Outside these depths the water deepens westward over a muddy bottom, where are from 80 to 90 and even 100 fathoms of water. Fishing here is mainly by trawl and gill nets.

Lying about SE. by S. ½ 5. from the Isle of Shoals 20 miles, 13 miles S. by W. from the whistling buoy on Jeffreys, and 43 miles S. by W. from Cape Elizabeth is a broken piece of bottom having from 75 to 85 fathoms of water over it, which is a haddock ground from January to April and a cusk and hake ground all the year.

A small shoal in the western part of the Cove of Jeffreys, having 50 fathoms over a bottom of blue clay and rocks and rising from the 60 and 70 fathom soundings about it, is about 1½ miles long by about 3/4 mile wide. This shoal is SSE. from Boon Island 15 miles. It is a winter ground for cod and haddock.

Clay Ridge. At various points about the edges of Jeffreys Ledge are small detached ridges, which in their season are good fishing grounds. The present piece of ground lies 26 miles S. by W. from the lightship at Portland, which course and distance bring us to the northern edge. There is a 50-fathom shoal of small size upon it, but elsewhere soundings average from 65 to 70 fathoms over a bottom of hard clay. The length of the ground is about 4 miles NNE. and SSW., and the breadth about 1 mile. This furnishes good haddocking in January, February. and March. the latter month showing the best fishing.

Jerry Yorks Ridge. This lies just inside and paralleling Jeffreys Ledge WNW. from its shoal water and about 5 miles distant from the ledge and about 18 miles SE. by S. ½ S. from Cape Porpoise. This ground has from 45 to 48 fathoms of water on a rocky broken bottom. It is about 5 miles long, NNE. and SSW., and averages 1½ miles wide. This is a good cod and haddock ground In the fall and up to January, these fish returning here in the spring months.

Howard Nunans Ridge. Of similar nature to the last, this rises 4 miles inside of and parallel to it, lying 14 miles from Cape Porpoise on the same bearings (SE. by S. ½ S.). This appears to be made up of two shoals, the northern rising to 50 fathoms of water over a rocky, broken bottom about 3 miles long by 1 mile wide, deepening southwesterly to a narrow, muddy gully, where are 80 fathoms, and rising again to 60 fathoms over rocks and broken ground. The whole ground is about 8 miles long with average widths of from 1 to 1½ miles. This ground furnishes good cod fishing and haddocking in the fall and early winter and again in the spring months.

Southeast Jeffreys. Off the southeast edge of Jeffreys, about 24 miles SE. from Boon Island, lies a piece of fishing ground having a hard bottom of sand, gravel, and rocks, where depths slope away gradually from the 50-fathom soundings near the main body of the bank to the 90-fathom mark farther out. This area is a good ground for cod and haddock in the winter and spring and a hake ground in March. This fishing spot is about 3 or 4 miles square and is bounded on all but the western side by muddy bottom, which is of little value as a fishing ground. Usually there is good haddocking in March on the outside of Jeffreys, on its southeastern edge and in the cove between it and Tillies in 60 and 70 fathom depths on a broken and muddy bottom. This spot lies SE ½ from the Isle of Shoals, 27 miles to the center.

Eastern Shoal Water of Cape Ann. This is generally considered a part of Jeffreys and is often spoken of as West Jeffreys by the fishermen. It extends In an ENE. direction from Cape Ann for a distance of from 15 to 18 miles. It is, in fact, a southwest continuation of Jeffreys Ledge, the two forming a nearly continuous ridge running NE. from Cape Ann a distance of about 42 miles. Depths on the so-called Eastern Shoal Water vary from 20 to 45 fathoms, the bottom being of rocks, pebbles, and coarse gravel over most of its extent. Sand and mud occur on the edges. The eastern part of the ground is resorted to by the haddock fleet during the fall and early winter, and other parts are visited more or less during the entire year for cod, haddock, and pollock by vessels and boats from Cape Ann and by craft of various types from Boston and Portland-line trawlers, gill-netters, and a few of the new type of small otter trawlers, this latter fleet of craft constantly growing in number.

On the ledge cod, haddock, and cusk are taken in the full winter and spring, winter, perhaps, furnishing the best fishing. There are also more or less pollock, and hake constitute an important part of the catch. In those seasons when herring make their appearance in these waters the seiners make good catches here, mostly of food fish, as the large herring are termed by the trade. The mackerel, also, appear on these grounds and on the smaller grounds nearer to shore to northward and westward in good-sized schools, usually from July 1 through September. For many years the haddock catch from this bank has been of considerable importance, and this statement remains true for recent years as well.

Formerly this fishery was almost entirely carried on by trawlers and hand-liners, but the gill-net fishery on these grounds is of great and steadily growing importance. Of late the larger part of the haddock catch has been taken by the "otter-trawl" method, this gear being operated by steamers of considerable size and upon the more distant grounds, such as Georges Bank, the South Channel, and the Western Bank. The same change to fishing grounds farther offshore has to a great extent taken place in the fleet of larger sailing vessels, thus leaving Jeffreys and other inshore banks to the smaller craft; except that, with the high prices of haddock and cod in the winter months, it is often profitable for these larger vessels to run off to near-by banks for one set and return to port the same day.

On the inner parts of this ground, particularly, the gill-net fleet operates extensively, mainly in the full and spring, on northwest Jeffreys 8 to 12 miles E. and SE. from Thacher Island, where the bottom is sand and rocks. Other gill-netting grounds are 8 to 15 miles NE. by E. from Thacher Island in 22 fathoms on a hard bottom of mud and mixed material of sand and gravel. The Cove of Jeffreys, NE. by E. 12 to 15 miles from Thacher Island, is a favorite haddock ground in the spring (April 20 to May 15) in 45 to 70 or even 80 fathoms, although gill nets are not often fished in more than 50 fathoms because of the, weight of the nets in the deeper water. In the spring (in April and May), the haddock come in on Scantum, 10 miles NNE. from Thacher Island between Jeffreys Ledge and the Isle of Shoals, on a broken bottom of rocks and blue clay in 55 to 70 fathoms.

Off Newburyport and N. and SW. of the Isle of Shoals are gill-netting grounds that are much used. Trawling and netting are carried on, beginning in 40 fathoms in February and March and working off to 70 fathoms off Salisbury Bench in May. Cod are on this ground about two weeks in October and in February and March are found in abundance off Boars Head. Hake are present here all the fall and are found all along the southeast side of these grounds in depths of 45 to 60 fathoms. A certain amount of halibut may be taken in most years at various points on a bottom of hard gravel in spring and early summer in 35 to 65 fathoms. In most years a large amount of mackerel is taken on Jeffreys, notably so in 1925. Herring, also, are usually abundant here in "herring years".

The Shoal Ground, stretching easterly from Thacher Island, has depths from 20 to 30 fathoms over a bottom of sand and gravel. This area is about 15 miles long by 5 miles wide and is an important pollock ground in their spawning time as well as a good fall cod-fishing ground. It is about 12 miles E. by N. from Thacher Island to its center and 21 miles SE. by S. from the Isle of Shoals. Flounder draggers also operate here on the shoal ground and all around Thacher Island but mostly to eastward & southeastward.

Tillies Bank. [13] This bears E & S from Eastern Point Light just dropping Thacher Island Light, then 3 miles farther for best fishing: and E. by S. ½ S.

from Thacher Island, Cape Ann, from which the shoal on the center of the ground is distant 18 miles. This is a small rocky spot with depths of from 25 to 28 fathoms, outside of which the water deepens to 40 fathoms over a considerable area. The length of the entire ground is about 10 miles in an E. and W. direction and the width about 5 miles. At the edge it falls off rapidly to depths of 50 to 60 fathoms before reaching the mud at still greater depths but an area of shoal water connects this ground with West Jeffreys. The bottom is rocky and rough over the greater part of the bank. Tillies was formerly regarded as one of the best fishing grounds off Cape Ann and is still resorted to for cod and haddock in the spring and fall; for hake in the spring, summer, and fall, and for pollock in the spring and fall. The fishing is mainly by trawling, with the gillnetters operating on the shoal grounds in less than 50 fathoms.

Stellwagen Bank also called Middle Bank. This separates Massachusetts Bay from the open water of the Gulf of Maine and extends from near Cape Ann nearly to Cape Cod. The center of this ground bears S by E ½ E from Thacher Island and N by W ½ W from Highland Light, Cape Cod. The Southern Part of the Bank is distant 5½ miles from Race Point Cape Cod, and its northwest prong reaches to within 12 or 15 miles of Eastern Point Cape Cod. The shoaler portion, with depths from 9½ to 19 fathoms, is 17½ miles long in a N by W and S by E direction and has a width of 4 miles. This part is sandy but the eastern slope, in depths of from 25 to 55 fathoms, consists of coarse sand gravel and pebbles. On this gravelly slope cod and haddock have been taken plentifully over a long term of years, the cod in the fall and spring and the haddock in the winter months. On the southern end of the bank and between this and Race Point cod abound in fall and winter. The whole bank is also a mackerel ground when the fish are in these waters, the best in the season averaging to be from July 15 through September.

This bank is now mainly an Italian boat ground and is used by small craft from Boston and Gloucester. Gill-netting here is especially extensive in November and December, mostly for pollock. Netters operate about 22 miles SSE. from Eastern Point in 22 to 25 fathoms on a hard bottom. Good pollock catches are made in 25 to 40 fathoms on the eastern and southeastern slopes in the latter part of November and early December. Haddock are here from November 1 to March 1 and from April 20 to May 15. Cod are present all the year, the largest school occurring during August, September and October. It is a cusk ground from November to March in the deeper water. What seems a somewhat unusual occurrence in these later years was the appearance of a considerable school of halibut on the northern slope of Stellwagen during the last half of April 1926, several small craft getting from 2,000 to 3,000 pounds in their fares.

Wild Cat Ridge. Very heavy tides sweep over this ground, making it difficult to haul gear in fishing upon it, whence, it is said, comes the name. It lies NNE from Highland Light, Cape Cod, 18 miles to its southern edge; SE ½ S from Thacher Island 31 miles; and is about 7½ miles long in a north and south direction by about 3½ miles wide. The bottom is hard, of broken shells and sand, and depths are from 45 to 60 fathoms. There are 100 fathom depths inside of the ground and from 100 to 110 fathoms outside of it. Apparently, this is an all the year ground for cod, cusk, and haddock, although but little fished at any time other than the winter seasons.

**Table 3—Outer Fishing Grounds,
showing the principle species taken upon them.**

Fishing ground	Cod	Haddock	Hake	Pollock	Cusk	Halibut	Herring	Mackerel	Lobsters	Miscellaneous
Grand Manan Bank	x	x	x	x		x	[1] x			
Middle Ground	x	x	x	x		x	[1] x			
Marblehead Bank	x	x	x	x	x	x				
German Bank	x	x	x	x	x	x				
Newfound	x		x		x					
Jones Ground	x		x	x	x					
Bank Comfort	x		x		x					
Clay Bank	x		x							
Newfound (off Jeffreys Bank)	x		x		x	x				
Jeffreys Bank	x	x		x	x	x				
Toothaker Ridge	x		x	x	x					
Cashes Bank	x	x	x		x	x	[1] x			
Ridge east of Cashes	x				x					
Ridge east of Cashes	x		x		x					
Ridge northwest of Cashes	x	x	x		x	x	[1] x			
Cashes Big Ridge	x	x	x		x	x	[1] x			
Ridge north of Georges	x				x					
John Dyers Ridge	x		x		x					
Fifty-five Fathom Bunch	x									
Fippenies Bank	x	x	x		x	x	[1] x			
Ridge south of Fippenies	x	x	x		x					
Maurice Lubees Ground	x	x	x		x					
Harvey Blacks Ridge	x	x	x	x	x					
Cod Ridge	x	x	x		x					
Three-Dory Ridge	x									
Platts Bank; New Ledge	x	x	x	x	x	x	[1] x			
Jeffreys Ledge	x	x	x	x	x	x	[1] x	x		
Cove west of Jeffreys	x	x	x		x					
Clay Ridge	x	x								
Jerry Yorks Ridge	x	x								
Howard Nunans Ridge	x	x								
Southeast Jeffreys	x	x	x							
Southeast Cove (Jeffreys and Tillies)		x								
Scantum		x								
Eastern Shoal Water	x	x	x	x	x	x	[1] x	x		[2] x
Shoal Ground	x	x		x						[2] x
Tillies Bank	x	x	x	x						
Stellwagen, Middle Bank	x	x	x	x	x	x	[1] x	x		
Wild Cat Ridge	x	x			x					

[1] Food fish. [2] Flounders.

GEORGES AREA

East side of Cape Cod. The sea bottom off the east side of Cape Cod is mainly sandy and slopes off gradually from the beach, reaching depths of 30 to 40 fathoms at 5 to 7 miles from land. Below Chatham the slope is even more gradual. Within these limits good catches of cod are taken occasionally, and to a less extent the same is true of haddock. Farther from the shore, in from 40 to 80 fathoms and from a point 8 or 10 miles off the Highlands of Cape Cod to another point lying 20 miles or more SSE. from Chatham Lights, is a continuous stretch of excellent haddock grounds for winter fishing. The deep water off Chatham furnishes excellent hake fishing in summer and fall.

This shore furnishes excellent mackerel fishing during most of the season when these fish are in northern waters. Virtually no gill-netters operate here, the distance to market being great and the chance of rough weather and the lack of safe harbor making it dangerous for small craft. From this stretch of shore (mostly from off Chatham) there were landed at Boston in the year 1923, 66 fares with a total of 1,797,826 pounds valued at $76,875.

Tobins. A name given to a piece of ground about 20 miles square lying S. by E. from the Highland Light. It runs from about 40 miles to about 60 miles offshore, the depths gradually increasing as the bottom slopes away evenly from the shore from 75 to 95 fathoms over a bottom of clay, sand, and pebbles. Cod are taken here in the spring, summer, and fall, and haddock in February, March, and April. A few hake are taken here in summer, but, as compared with the grounds off Chatham, this is not to be considered a hake ground.

Morris Ledge. This lies eastward of Chatham and is a favorite ground for certain cod fishermen during spring and early summer. Schooners and small craft operate here.

Outer Crab Ledge. The center lies about 14 miles ESE from Chatham Lights. It extends about 5 or 6 miles in a N. and S. direction and is about 1 mile wide. Depths run from 19 to 23 fathoms; the bottom is rocky. The fishing is principally for cod in the fall, winter and spring. Vessel fishing here is principally in the spring.

Nantucket Shoals. This stretch of bars and deeper waters between, roughly triangular in form with its apex at the north, lies along the western edge of the South Channel, extending S. and SE. from the southern end of Cape Cod and Nantucket Island. From Monomoy Point to Rogers Fishing Ground, on the eastern edge of Phelps Bank, it is SSE. 80 miles. Its width from Southeast Rips to the western edge of New South Shoal is 40 miles. The area includes a number of "fishing spots" and shoals, among which the following are the most important: Pollock Rip Ground, Rose and Crown Shoal, Great Rip, Davis Bank, Fishing Rip, Old and New South Shoal, and Phelps Bank.

On and about all these shoals the sail fleet makes good catches, mainly consisting of cod but with a fair proportion of pollock, also, and in the deeper water close to them, in spring and summer, a considerable amount of haddock. An occasional large halibut is taken, and even good catches have been reported. There were noted in the daily report of the Boston Fish Bureau between May 15 and August 15, 1920, 10 trips made by the smaller vessels of the halibut fleet that landed fares of from 2,000 to 10,000 pounds of this species from this area. Perhaps more would be taken if the halibut fishery were to be followed here as in other areas. "Rip fishing," as conducted here, is done "at a drift," moving over the shoals and, as they move off from them, sailing back to repeat the process. The fish are taken by hand-lining with "cockle" bait or by "jigging" the fish with a shiny piece of metal representing a herring or similar fish, below which are set twin hooks, the fish being struck when it is felt investigating the lure. This fishery generally is carried on during May, June, July, and August. In the mackerel and herring seasons these grounds usually furnish good fishing for these species, the fish usually striking here from May 15 to July 15.

Pollock Rip Grounds. These lie between Pollock Rip Lightship and Shovelful Lightship and extend northward to Pollock Rip Shoal. These grounds are 3 miles long, E. and W., by 2 miles N. and S. The depths range from 4 to 12 fathoms. These are fished from Monomoy and in stormy weather from Chatham instead of going to the Crab Ledge. Late in the spring and early in the fall the cod move inshore. In winter the cod leave Pollock Rip for the deeper water.

Rose and Crown Shoal. This is a small piece of ground 7 miles ESE. from Sankaty Head. The fishing area lies between the Round Shoal and Rose and Crown buoys, making a stretch perhaps 6 miles long by 1½ miles wide. Sometimes good fishing may be had from 6 to 12 mile, from Great Round Shoal buoy. As elsewhere on and about these shoals, the cod is the principal species caught, pollock being next in importance, and a few haddock.

Nantucket Shoals, Madisons Spot. SSE. 13 miles front Round Shoal buoy, has 9 fathoms over a smooth hard bottom of sand. It is about 3 miles long, from SE. to NW. by 1½ miles wide. This is a flounder ground for the greater part of the year and a good cod ground in October and November. As is the rule elsewhere in this neighborhood, tides are heavy over this ground.

Nantucket Shoal—Great Rip. Lies 13 miles E. by S. ½ S. from Sankaty Head Light. Nantucket. It is 5 miles long from N, to S. and 3 miles broad. Over this area the depths are from 9 to 18 feet, but the fishing is done mainly around the edges in 6 to 12 fathoms where the bottom is gravel and shells covered with sponges and kelp. Here, as on all these shoals, the greater part of the fishing is done by that method known as "rip fishing." Cod are taken chiefly by hand-lining in May. June, July, and August.

Nantucket Shoals; Davis Bank; Crab Bank. This is an irregular piece of bottom lying in a generally ENE. and WSW direction at about 20 miles distance ESE from Sankaty Head. It is perhaps 14 miles long by 5 miles wide at its broadest. Depths upon it are from 4 to 9 fathoms, with soundings of 12 to 18 about it, over a bottom of sand and broken shells.

Nantucket Shoals Fishing Rip is an elongate bank lying 29 miles SE. from Sankaty Head Light. It is 10 miles long in a NE and SW direction and Southeast Rip (Nantucket Shoals) lies SE. from Sankaty Head 35 miles. It has depths from 8 to 10 fathoms over an area about 10 miles long by 2 miles wide, with from 22 to 30 fathoms over the sandy bottom around it.

Phelps Bank. This bank lies 38 miles SE, ½ S. from Sankaty Head Light and agrees more or less in size, shape, trend, and character of the bottom with Fishing Rip. Depths are from 10 to 17 fathoms. On the southeast edge of this lies Rogers Fishing Ground, with 24 to 40 fathoms over fine gray sand. It is perhaps mainly a haddock ground.

Nantucket Shoals (South Shoal). This name is applied to the fishing ground about Nantucket Lightship, which marks the Old South Shoal and the New South Shoal, the two making a continuous reef of irregular form some 10 to 12 miles in length and from 1 to 3 miles wide. The northern end of this lies about 12 miles S. by E. from Sankaty Head (the Old South Shoal), and the southern extremity of the New South Shoal reaches to about 20 miles S. ½ E. from the same point. The fishing ground lies mostly to the S. of these shoals and about the lightship, where otter trawling is carried on in all directions from the ship except from N. to NE., where lie the vessels sunk by the German submarine in the late war. This fishery is also carried on WNW. from the ship for a distance of 40 miles, even into 7 fathom depths near Muskeget Inlet.

Elsewhere depths average from 13 to 18 fathoms on the inner parts of the grounds, whence they slope away gradually from the shore soundings into 50, 80, or even more on the outer edge, where the ground falls away rapidly into the deeps. For the most part this area has a bottom of sand, but there are small stretches of coarse gravel, broken shells, pebbles, and a few muddy spots.

Within comparatively recent years this ground has been much used by the otter trawlers, which type of craft has developed a productive fishery here, which is being operated in steadily increasing volume and takes a catch that is predominantly of haddock.

The proportion of cod taken here by these vessels is very small, even smaller than that from other grounds fished by the otter-trawl method. Pollock and hake, too, make a small item in the fares from the neighborhood of the South Shoal. In the average otter-trawl fare haddock makes up the greater part of the catch because, as a rule, this type of gear is operated mostly on the smooth, sandy bottom which this species prefers. The otter-trawl fishery here is at its best from early May through June, July, and the first halt of August. Few trips are reported from this ground at other seasons. Perhaps the haddock leaves the shoal grounds here earlier than when it moves out of the same depths in The Channel.

The early fishing for the swordfish generally takes place in this vicinity, and in normal seasons mackerel are found here in abundance from May 15 to August, and, as is the custom with this uncertain fish, it may appear here again in the late fall.

The Channel. [14] The Channel marks the western edge of Georges Bank. Its boundaries are somewhat indefinite, but the old Eldridge chart states that for the fishermen the 30 fathom curve running southerly from Race Point. Cape Cod, limits its western edge. This ground is much visited by the Boston fleet, both sail and steam, line trawlers and otter trawlers, the fleet of Gloucester, and the otter-trawl fleet that has developed in New York in recent years. This area is all good fishing ground in the proper season, but perhaps the most important is that part lying 25 miles E. ½ S. from Sankaty Head, Nantucket. Here is a level, sandy bottom, where, during May, June, July, and August, the otter trawlers operate successfully in 18 to 30 fathoms of water, making a catch that consists principally of haddock, with a considerable proportion of cod, especially in June and July, and with a fair amount also of pollock, cusk, and hake. Small halibut are fairly abundant here, also, these fish being of from 5 to R pounds, rarely larger.

Flounders are abundant, with a good number of "lemon soles" and "gray soles," which are very popular with the trade.

The sail fleet operates here also, but, as a rule, more of these vessels are found on the ground lying some 10 miles farther eastward, on the edge of Georges in somewhat deeper water (30 to 50 fathoms) on a rougher and rockier bottom, where there is a greater proportion of cod in the catch than on the western area.

The Sankaty Head ground is about 20 miles long by about 8 miles wide, stretching from 55 miles SE. from Highland Light to 78 miles SE. by S ½ S. from the same point (the bottom of the Channel), and is bounded on all sides by pieces of bottom less favorable to the operation of the otter trawl because of the presence of rocks, sponges, or other obstacles, which interfere with the free passage of the net over the bottom but offer less trouble to the line-trawl fishermen. A good spring haddock ground lies ESE. 65 miles from the Highlands in 70 fathoms. best in March and April. As the cold weather advances the fish move away in great part from these grounds, going into the deeper water, the catches of the fall and winter months being taken mainly In depths of from 60 to 100 fathoms. At this season and in these depths the vicinity of the Corner of the Channel, Clarks Side. and the area N and W of the Cultivator usually have a good winter school of haddock. This has been particularly large during the past three year. (1923 to 1925). Thus, it may be seen that the Channel is an important ground during most of the year.

The figures of the catch from Clarks Bank have been shown together with those of Georges Bank. of which, in fact, this area is a part.

The larger part of the sail fleet is found fishing on the grounds of the eastern side of the Channel and of the western edge of Georges Bank, in part to escape the damage that the otter trawlers cause to them in dragging away their gear. It is often impossible for these steamers to avoid some damage of this kind: especially is this the case in the thick weather so prevalent oil Georges. In the summer months of the "mackerel years" a large catch of this species is taken from the waters of the Channel.

St. Georges Bank, more generally known as Georges Bank. [15] This is by far the largest and most important fishing ground near the coast of the United States and is second to none in the western Atlantic except the Grand Bank of Newfoundland. It lies eastward of Cape Cod and Nantucket Shoals and is apparently an extension of the latter, since the water is no deeper between the southern part of the shoals and the western part of the bank than in many places upon it. Its southern limit, as shown on the chart, is 40° 40′ north latitude, though the 50-fathom line extends 7 miles farther south. The southern limit, therefore, may be considered to be about 40° 30′ and the northern as 42° 08′ north latitude. The eastern part is in about 66° and the western in about 69° west longitude. The greatest length from the northeastern to the southwestern extremity is about 150 miles; the greatest width, N. and S., about 98 miles, according to the charts of the Coast Survey.

Depths range from 2 to 50 fathoms. On the western part, between the parallels of 41° 10′ and 41° 53′ north latitude and the meridians of 87° 20′ and 68° 37′ west longitude are a number of shoals, known as the East Shoal, North Shoal, Southwest Shoal. Cultivator, etc. The Southwest Shoal is the largest, being 15 miles long SSW and NNE., with an average width of 2½ miles. The position of the center of this shoal is 41° 39′ north latitude and 67° 48′ west longitude. There are from 2 to 15 fathoms of water on the shoals and between them are depths of from 12 to 30 fathoms. The tide sweeps over these with great force, causing strong rips, and during rough weather the sea breaks heavily on them, rendering approach to their vicinity extremely hazardous.

Over most of the bank the bottom is sand, although patches of rough ground (gravel, pebbles, and rocks) of greater or less extent are found in some localities. Its position between the Bay of Fundy and the Gulf Stream cause the tide to run swifter than on other banks and to swirl around instead of passing directly over, back and forth. The writer has seen two men have difficulty in holding an empty dory against the current.

The Report on the Fishery Industry of the United States, in 1887, says that the first attempt at fishing here (of which there is any record) was made in 1821 by three Gloucester vessels. The cod and halibut industry, according to the same authority, began in 1830, although not fully established as a permanent industry until 1835.

The area of the whole bank is approximately 8,050 square miles, all of which, except for the shoals, is available in summer for the taking of cod, haddock, cusk, halibut, and hake, with a considerable amount of mackereling and swordfishing, as well as the taking of other species.

During February, March, and April large schools of cod make their appearance on the bank. At this season these are found most abundantly on the "Winter Fishing Ground"; a part of Georges lying eastward and southeastward of the North Shoal between the parallels of 41° 30′ and 42° 00′ north latitude and 66° 38′ and 67° 30′ west longitude. The area of this Winter Fishing Ground is about 1,100 square miles. This part of the bank seems entirely given over to the codfish, since it is too broken, sharp, and rocky to please the haddock. Depths here are from 30 to 40 fathoms, deepening away from the North Shoal. This area is essentially a spawning ground for the cod, which appear to come on the hank from the SE., as they almost invariably, after reaching the ground, move slowly to the N. and W. as spring approaches. This is in the direction of the shoals. As soon as the spawning season is over the schools of cod break up, but more or less fish are caught on different parts of the ground at all times of the year, though rarely are they found so plentiful as when the winter school is on the ground. Cod are found along the Northern Edge virtually the year around, though many of the winter school move on to the inner waters of the gulf and others go over to Browns Bank, where the early comers seem to appear in the first days of April.

In its production Georges Bank itself is rather evenly divided between haddock and cod, the cod showing a slightly larger proportion. The South Channel, on the western edge of Georges, shows predominantly as a haddock ground, and the haddock from The Channel is considered a better fish than that from Georges. Georges Bank itself is also an important haddock ground in the spring and early summer, when this species abounds about the Cultivator Shoal (SE. by S. 88 miles from Highland Light. Cape Cod) in depths from 18 to 30 fathoms; and at the same season along the Northern Edge (140 to 200 miles E. by S. ½ S. from Boston Lightship in about 41° to 42° N. lat. and 66° to 88° W. long.) in 45 to 80 fathoms in summer, the fish moving off into the deeper water (90 to 100 fathoms) in the neighborhood of the Corner of the Channel as the winter comes on. Many are found in March, when they return from the deep water, when fishing is carried on 65 miles SE. from Highland in 70 fathoms; then they come into the 40-fathom depths from the North Shoal westward to the Corner of The Channel along the Northern Edge. In April the Cultivator Cove is good ground even into 20-fathom depths.

The Southwest Part. (120 miles SSE. from Highland Light, Cape Cod, with 45 to 80 fathom depths) is a good ground for haddock from the beginning of the fall up to about Christmas, after which the best winter fishing for this species is found on the Southeast Part (reached by steaming 145 miles ESE. from Boston Lightship in order to clear the shoals, then SSE.

40 to 50 miles, depending upon what part of the ground it is desired to fish). January is perhaps the best fishing month upon this portion of Georges.

While not considered a halibut ground, as compared with some of the other offshore banks, Georges can show a very considerable catch of this species. Because of its nearness to the markets it is more intensely fished than any other ground of equal area and by a far greater variety of crafts, most of which take a greater or less amount of halibut. The otter-trawl fleet, both here and in The Channel, takes a large amount of this species when its total catch is considered; and these fish are mainly small, of from 4 to 10 pounds in weight, with only rarely a larger one. The salt fishers, also, and the rest of the market fleet combine to make an imposing total of the poundage of halibut from Georges and its vicinity. The Georges halibut is esteemed by the trade above the halibut from other grounds. Perhaps its flesh may be superior, though for what reason it is difficult to say, unless because, since the trips to this ground average fewer days in length, the fish are received in the markets in a fresher condition than are those from more distant banks.

The principal halibut grounds on Georges for the spring and summer months (April to July) lie between the Cultivator Shoal and the North Shoal in depths from 10 to 18 fathoms, and E., S., and SW. from the North Shoal in the same soundings. This area is sometimes called Little Georges. There are also a number of mussel grounds on the southwest part of Georges, having depths averaging 20 fathoms, all of which furnish good feeding grounds and a substantial catch of halibut in the seasons when these fish are in the shoal water.

During July and August the halibut are found along the Northern Edge, over a stretch of ground about 65 miles long in 60 to 100 fathoms; and from this time until the hard weather of the winter begins the fishing goes on about the Northeast Peak (about 42° 00′ N. and 66° 00′ W.) over the narrow area on the edge of the suddenly deepening water, beginning in from 60 to 70 fathoms, then out to 200 and even 300 fathoms. The winter fishing on Georges is very difficult and somewhat hazardous, so that the halibut fishery in these waters is rarely carried on or, at best, by very few vessels after November or before March.

Mackerel are usually quite abundant on Georges in their season, generally being large or medium fish. Herring also are found there in good number but are somewhat distant from market as fresh fish.

Table 4—Fishing grounds of the Georges area, showing the principal species taken upon them.

Fishing grounds	Cod	Haddock	Hake	Pollock	Cusk	Halibut	Herring	Mackerel	Lobsters	Miscellaneous
East side of Cape Cod	x	x	x				x	x		
Tobins	x	x	x					x		
Morris Ledge	x									
Outer Crab Ledge	x									
Nantucket Shoals	x	x		x		x		x		
Pollock Rip Grounds	x			x						
Rose and Crown	x	x		x						
Madisons Spot	x									[1] x
Great Rip	x			x						
Davis Bank; Crab Bank	x			x						
Fishing Rip	x			x						
Southeast Rip	x			x						
Phelps Bank	x	x		x				x		
South Shoal	x	x	x	x				x		[2] x
The Channel	x	x	x	x	x	x		x		[2] x
Georges Bank	x	x	x	x	x	x	x	x		[2] x

[1] Soles, lemon and gray.   [2] Swordfish and soles.

By far the largest percentage of the swordfish catch landed in the ports of Boston, Gloucester, and Portland comes from Georges Bank. A considerable portion of the fish listed from this ground under the heading "Miscellaneous" is made up of this species.

The swordfish arrive on Georges on the Southwest Part and on the Southern Edge about June 5, and the traveling schools pass over the bank, northward bound, up to August 10. In fact, all through the season when they are present in northern waters, even up to November, they may be found on Georges. Probably the best area of the bank for this species is on the parallel of 41° N., where the shoal rises steeply out of "blue water."

OFFSHORE BANKS

Browns Bank. This bank lies in a northeastern direction from Georges and is separated from it by a gully 15 miles wide, in which the depths range from 100 to 450 fathoms. Its area is about 2,275 square miles. The greatest length, from SE to NW, is 63 miles and the greatest width is 43 miles. It is situated between 64° 52" and 68° 29" west longitude, and 41° 50" and 43° 02" north latitude. There is a small rocky shoal on the northern part, on which, it is said, there is not 9 to 15 fathoms. The bank slopes away from the shoal, S. and E. to depths of 55 to 75 fathoms, but at a distance of 12 or 15 miles off, it again rises to 30 to 50 fathoms. This area of shoal water, within the 50 fathom limit, is 50 miles long and has an average width of 15 miles. North of the shoal the water deepens suddenly to 70 and 80 fathoms. The bottom is largely coarse sand, gravel, pebbles, and rocks and is rich in animal life. The area of the bank is approximately 1,370 square geographical miles.

Tides here are quite as strong as on the eastern side of Georges Bank, the ebb having an average strength of 1 1/3 miles an hour and the flood is somewhat stronger. The greatest strength of the flood tide sets W. the ebb in nearly an opposite direction.

Haddock, cod, cusk, halibut, pollock and hake are the principal food fishes procured from this bank, ranking in volume in the order named. In value, however, halibut takes third place in the list. Cod are plentiful here in winter, though fewer vessels fish here than on Georges Bank, at that season. At other seasons the codfishery on Browns Bank compares favorably with that of other banks in the vicinity. Cod are present the year around, in May and June feeding in depths of about 40 fathoms, going into 80 fathoms in August, and into depths of about 100 fathoms in cold weather.

Haddock, also, are present all the year, the period of greatest abundance being usually January and February. In March and April they are most abundant in 27 to 30 fathoms; at other seasons they are in 50 fathoms and deeper, especially in winter, when generally they can be found in 80 to 100 fathoms. Cusk are present in the deep water all the year.

Older reports say (1880-81): "Halibut were formerly found here in abundance, but at present the fishery is limited to an occasional trip off the southern and western edge." It will be noted that a fair amount of halibut was taken here during 1923, when this bank ranked third in volume of halibut taken, which seems a good showing when the comparatively small size of the ground is considered. Fairly good catches have been made SW from the Northwest Peak of Browns, about 66° 50′ west longitude and 42° 40′ north latitude, along the 100-fathom curve and following eastward to the southward of La Have and beyond, perhaps to 63° west longitude. The Southeast Peak is perhaps the most productive of the halibut grounds here, "setting" off from the shoaler parts into the narrow deep-water channel between this and Georges perhaps 20 miles distant.

A considerable part of the fish listed under the heading "Miscellaneous" are swordfish, which come upon this bank during their summer wanderings.

It will be noted that the number of otter-trawl fares from this ground is small. It is only in recent years that this method of fishing has been employed here, the bottom having been thought to be too rough for the successful operation of gear of this type upon it.

Seal Island Ground. This is called also on the charts in its northwest part, the German Bank and lies off the western part of Nova Scotia. Very few charts show it, as it is somewhat difficult to define its exact limits. It is a direct continuation of the shore soundings, which slope gradually from the land to the S. and W. and continue in a northerly direction beyond what might be considered the bounds of the grounds. To the S. it extends nearly to Browns Bank, from which it is separated by a narrow gully 70 to 80 fathoms deep. To the N. it reaches 38 miles beyond Seal Island and to the NW. about 35 miles from the same island. The southern limit of the ground is in 43° and the northern 43° 45′ north latitude, while the western boundary may be placed at 66° 40′ west longitude. The entire ground outside the 3 mile limit covers an area of 1,250 miles.

There is a small shoal called Pollock Rip, with a depth of 7 fathoms, bearing SW from Seal Island, distant 9½ miles; but otherwise the ground slopes quite gradually, the depths being from 15 to 70 fathoms. The bottom is mainly coarse gravel and pebbles with occasional rocky spots of greater or less extent. The tides sweep over this ground with considerable force out from and in toward the Bay of Fundy. the flood running strongest.

In general, the species of fish found here and the seasons of their greatest abundance are much as on Browns Bank. The principal fishes taken are haddock, cod, cusk, halibut, and hake, and a very small amount of pollock. Except for the haddocking, the best fishing season is from March to October. Halibut are said to have been very plenty here in the past but are said to have been comparatively rare in recent years, although occasional good fares are brought from these grounds, perhaps more commonly in the spring and early summer and a few at other seasons.

In April they are found most commonly in 80 fathom depths; in May in 30 to 40 fathoms, in June the best halibuting is had in 25-fathom depths or even in shoaler water. (The halibut catch shown for the year chosen (1927) is unusually small, most years yielding a fair amount of this species from this ground. Apparently no member of the American halibut fleet visited this ground for the year.)

Cod are present here the year around, perhaps the best fishing taking place in May and June, when the fish are found in about 40 fathoms They go into deeper water, about 60 fathoms, in August and into 100 fathoms as the cold weather advances. This Seal Island ground may be considered essentially as a feeding ground for the cod, which seem to appear here after the spawning season is over, to fatten upon the crabs and mollusks living on the bottom and on the herring and other small fish that swim back and forth In the tide rips.

Haddock are also present all the year, the schools being most abundant and the number greatest in January and February, when the fish are in about 50 to 60 fathoms. Apparently they come into depths of from 27 to 30 fathoms in March and April for spawning.

Cusk are present here during most of the year in 80 fathoms on the hard bottom. Pollock are few on this ground at any time of the year. This species, together with herring and mackerel, are abundant on the "shore soundings" of Seal Island Ground, whence, following the abundant food furnished by the smaller fish, they range a short distance in to the Bay of Fundy. Many mackerel are taken in the traps in the vicinity of Yarmouth, Nova Scotia, which seems to mark the limit of their penetration in any considerable schools on the western shore of Nova Scotia.

What is apparently a gradually deepening extension of Seal Island Ground is found about 65 miles SSE. from Mount Desert Rock and 60 miles W. from Seal Island. There seems to be no distinguishing name for this area.

The depths here are from 70 to 100 fathoms over a broken bottom of mud, gravel, and in places fine sand. The ground falls off rapidly on all sides except toward Seal Island and the Nova Scotia coast, leaving an area at its end of somewhat indeterminate length, perhaps 18 or 20, miles, and having a distance across of about 8 miles at its widest part.

Apparently there is no reason why this should not be an all-the-year fishing ground, but it seems not to be visited much in the winter. It furnishes, however, a very good summer handline fishery for cod at dogfish time, and in the spring months it abounds in cod, cusk, and hake, all fish of large size.

Roseway Bank. This bank lies N. of the western part of La Have and SE. of Shelbourne Light, Nova Scotia: 31 miles SSE. from the whistling buoy off Lockport, Nova Scotia, to the southeastern edge. It is oblong in shape and of small extent—about 270 square geographical miles. Its greatest length is 21 miles and its greatest breadth 15 miles. It extends from 43° 12′ to 43° 33′ north latitude, and from 64° 25′ to 64° 52′ west longitude and at the northwest corner is connected with the shore limit of 60 fathoms by a narrow neck. Depths are from 33 to 48 fathoms. The bottom is of sand, gravel, and rocks; on the Northeast Peak the bottom is of yellow mud and gravel.

Currents in this region are not nearly so strong as about Cape Sable and Browns Bank, their general direction being WSW. and ENE the westerly much the stronger, though the force and direction of both are much influenced by the winds.

The principal fish taken here are cod, haddock, and cusk, but hake, pollock and halibut occur, the best fishing months being from May to October, when the bank is resorted to by craft from western Nova Scotia. A few New England craft also fish here.

La Have Bank. Situated eastward of Browns Bank and S. and E. of Roseway Bank. It extends from 42° 34′ to 43° 26′ north latitude a distance of 52 miles, and from 63° 50′ to 65° 07′ west longitude a distance of about 54 miles. The bank is nearly divided into two portions, of which the eastern (La Have Bank proper) extends N and S. 39 miles and the western portion nearly E. and W. about 35 miles. The total area of the bank is about 1,200 miles.

The bottom is largely coarse gravel, pebbles, and rock, with smaller areas of sand distributed here and there. Depths run from 40 to 50 fathoms. The general set of the currents is to the westward, but this is much influenced by the force and direction of the wind and is generally quite strong during easterly blows.

The principal fishing upon this bank in the past has been for cod and haddock: and while former reports, (1881) speak of this as having once been a favorite fishing ground for halibut and state that it was not at time of much importance in that fishery, the figures for this ground for the year 1923 show the halibut catch to have been third in volume and first in value of the species taken there. In fact, the catch of halibut here makes quite an imposing figure when the comparatively small size of the ground is considered.

Little La Have and the La Have Ridges are simply continuations of this back toward the Western Bank for a distance of about 45 miles. This places the eastern limit in about 62° 50′ west longitude, the northern and southern boundaries being about as those of La Have Bank. The area of the ridges is about 1,575 miles. The bottom here is a succession of ridges of pebbles and gravel with occasional patches of rocks. Depths are from 53 to 80 fathoms. The current, occasionally strong, is weaker here than farther W. on the bank and, except during easterly winds, is but little noticed. The general set is westerly.

"The Ridges" says the report before mentioned, "were for a number of years one of the favorite resorts for halibut catchers in winter, and many good catches of cod were taken here at that season. At present but few halibut are caught except in the deep water along the southern edge of the ground, where they sometimes have been found quite plentiful during nearly the entire year." Apparently there has not been much change in these conditions since the writer's time; fish seem to be present here In about the same quantities as in former years.

One piece of bottom, having depths of 25 to 50 fathoms over red clay, lying approximately in 43° 08' to 43° 10' north latitude and about 81° to 83° west longitude, seems a good spring and early summer ground. Apparently red-clay bottom indicates a good halibut ground, as this species is usually present where such a bottom is found.

Hake are found in good numbers in the deep water about the edges of the ground and even on the Ridges.

These waters are quite heavily fished from Canadian ports, and a fair number of American vessels visit them each year, most of them hailing from Boston or Gloucester.

Scandinavian Bank. Eighteen miles SSW. from Shelbourne Light. Nova Scotia. It is about 3 miles long in an E. and W. direction by about ½ mile wide. In general, the bottom is level, with depths from 50 to 70 fathoms; the shoal parts are sharp and rocky, the bottom over the deeper portions being composed mostly of small black and yellow pebbles.

This is a summer halibut ground (July and August) in depths from 45 to 60 fathoms, and halibut occur in October in the deeper waters about it. It is also a fair summer cod ground, and cusk are present in the deep water about the edges during most of the year. In general, species and seasons are much as on Roseway.

Western Bank. This is one of the most important fishing grounds of the western Atlantic, whether as regards size or the abundance of its product. It lies S. of Cape Breton Island and the eastern part of Nova Scotia between the parallels of 42° 55' and 44° 46' north latitude and the meridians of 59°04' and 62° 35' west longitude. It has a length of 156 miles and a width, including the Middle Ground, of 76 miles. It is about 420 miles E. ½ S. from Boston to the southwestern edge, which means about 48 hours' steaming for the otter-trawl fleet.

The general contour of the bank within the 65-fathom line, as laid down on the Admiralty chart, approaches somewhat a very elongated ellipse, the longer axis running NE. by E. and SW. by W.; but over a broad area to eastward of the center of the bank, soundings of less than 50 fathoms connect it directly with the Middle Ground, which we have here included in the some bank. The total extent of the bank thus defined is about 7,000 square geographical miles. Off its eastern end lies Banquereau (the Quereau of the fishermen) with The Gully between, and a short distance of the western edge are the La Have Ridges.

The depths off the southern edge of the bank increase rapidly from 80 to 700, 1,200, and even 1,400 fathoms. At the eastern end is Sable Island, [16] "graveyard of ships", a long, narrow, crescent-shaped elevation seemingly lessening in area each year, formed entirely of sand that has been blown Into innumerable hummocks and dunes. Off both ends of the island are long and dangerous sand bars. The length of the island is 20 miles; its greatest width is about 1½ miles. It is said that the Northwest Light has been moved three times due to the fact that the western end of the island has been literally blown away. It lies in an E. and W. direction, and the depth of water over the bars for a distance of 7 to 10 miles out does not exceed 2 fathoms, and even 10 miles farther out the depths do not exceed 10 to 11 fathoms. Within recent years fishermen have reported the appearance of a sand shoal about 5 or 6 miles SE. from the Northeast Light. This is said to appear at low water.

In general, the bank slopes S. and W. from the island, depths ranging from 18 to 60 fathoms. The bottom is mostly sandy with patches of gravel and pebbles. Currents are sometimes very strong about Sable Island and are somewhat irregular; apparently they are much influenced by the winds. On the other parts of the bank usually there is but little current, whatever there is usually tending toward the west.

Formerly the cod and halibut were the food fishes most taken here, but with the changed methods in the fishery (as the growth of the otter-trawl fleet) and a changed taste in our public the haddock catch has become the second most important in the receipts of fish from these waters. The halibut fishery stands third in the list. Other bottom feeders occur in less numbers, the pollock and the cusk perhaps being next in order of importance, with hake and a considerable amount of the various flatfishes in the otter trawls. These latter are marketed as sole.

Noting the small amount of haddock in the fares taken from these waters in former years, the writer asked a number of old-time fishermen as to its abundance in the old days. The reply was usually "Oh, yes, there were always haddock there; sometimes they bothered us a lot." Then, noting my surprise at so putting it, "You know, the haddock isn't much as a salt fish."

It will be noted that in 1923 the haddock catch here was a very good second to the cod catch in poundage, though not so valuable proportionately. In the otter-trawl catch from this ground it will be noted that the positions of the two species are reversed. As a rule, these steamers certainly take more than 2 pounds of haddock to 1 of cod on other offshore grounds—perhaps the result of operating in the shoaler waters and on the smoother bottom because of the difficulty of dragging over the rocky and kelp-covered ground, which the cod seems to prefer. But the bottom on the Western Bank is of such nature as to offer little obstruction to the passage of the net, so that virtually all parts of it may be fished by this method; and this, added to the known movements of the cod schools makes it possible at certain seasons of the year to catch a larger proportion of this species if it is so desired.

Haddock are found about the bars at both ends of the island in March and from that time to about June 1 in from 15 to 22 fathoms. They are also abundant 18 miles W. from the Northwest Light at the same seasons and at the same depths. During April, May, and June they come in close to the island in from 10 to 17 fathoms—even to 1 fathom. Through the rest of the year (except for the colder months, when they have moved off into deeper water) they may be found all over the bank on sandy bottom in 28 to 30 fathoms, where most of the beam trawl fishing is carried on.

There is a good cod school each year on the comparatively level bottom along the western and southwestern edges of the ground in 70 fathoms and more from February 1 to May 1, and in most years a certain amount of this species is taken on this area. In May this school seems to have moved on to a piece of bottom about 20 miles long lying SW. from the Northwest Light and having depths averaging 27 fathoms. With fair fishing for cod on the Western Bank during most of the year, they seem to be most abundant from the first of March to June. The winter school here appears to be smaller than that on Georges, but apparently this species visits this ground in considerable numbers during the spawning season. In winter the cod are mainly found upon the western part of the bank, moving into the shoaler waters toward Sable Island as the spring advances (during March and April), the "Bend" of the island and the neighborhood of the bars in 2 to 4 fathoms, where they can be seen taking the hook or can be "jigged." being favorite grounds. The ground lying W. from the Northwest Light, on and about the Northwest

Bar (18 miles W, from the light), is a favorite cod ground in May and June. The shoal water over the rocky bottom WNW from the Northwest Light furnishes good cod fishing from June 10 to July 1. This piece begins just outside the 3-mile stretch of breakers running out from the land and extends offshore in a generally westerly direction to 24 fathoms. Much hand-lining is done here.

In the shoal water, in April and May, the fish seem to be feeding on the "lant," (Ammodytes americanus). It is said that the fish taken on the bottom close to the island are smaller than those found farther west. The shoal water of the northern shore of the island is said to have good cod grounds and favorite spots for "dory hand-lining." The cod schools seem to arrive on the Northern Peak (SE. from the Northeast Light 40 miles to SE ½ S. from same point 28 miles) in late March and the first of April, moving N. and W. to the island. The cod of Sable Island are said to be fine, firm fish, perhaps due to the abundance of the "red clams" (bank clams) on these grounds.

The cod and haddock fishery is carried on by American and Canadian sailing vessels and otter trawlers, an increasing number of English and French vessels of the latter class engaging in the fishery of this ground each year.

Halibut are found on the Western Bank virtually all the year at depths varying with the seasons. As a halibut bank, this, with The Gully and Quereau—in fact, all one piece of ground—ranks second only to the Grand Bank Itself. The best fishing here for halibut is found from January to October. There are numerous places on and about the bank that the halibut seems to prefer, as the Peak of Pike, 85 miles W. by S. from the Northwest Light of Sable Island; S. and SW. of Sable Island from 12 to 38 miles; SW. 20 miles in 60 fathoms in May; thence out into 100 and 150 fathoms in June; in fact, following the 100-fathom curve along the edge of this bank, past the Northeast Peak (40 miles SE. from the Northeast Light), into the Gully and around the Southern Prong of Quereau to the Middle Prong. Apparently they leave this piece of bottom in July. Often the fish are close to the island in the spring, where the water is so shoal that they can be seen taking the bait or playing with the hook before taking. In April, May, and June a good halibut ground is in 18 fathoms 24 miles WNW. from Sable Island.

The Western Bank seems to be a good feeding ground for both cod and halibut as it abounds in shellfish and crustaceans, and at certain periods there are many smaller species of fish upon it, such as the lant and herring, on which these species and the haddock, also, especially prey. A considerable amount of swordfish is taken here in August and September, mainly by American vessels.

Banquereau. Separated from the Western Bank by The Gully, this has a very irregular form—the main bank roughly rectangular, with a narrow westerly extension of comparatively regular form. Its length, E. and W., is about 120 miles, its greatest width about 47 miles, and its total area about 2,800 miles.

The main portion of the bank lies between 44° 04' and 45° 01' north latitude and 67° 10' and 59° 00' west longitude, and the western prolongation lies between 44° 24' and 44° 42' north latitude and 69° 00' and 80° 05' west longitude. North of Banquereau lies Artimon, distant 3 miles, and Misaine, distant from 2 to 15 miles according to the places from which measurements are taken. The currents here are of varying force, much influenced by the wind, so that several days of strong tides may be followed by intervals when there is little if any current.

On the eastern part of Quereau is an area of shoal ground called the Rocky Bottom, having a depth of about 18 fathoms; elsewhere depths run from 18 to 50 fathoms. For the most part the bottom is rocky, but there are scattered patches of sand and gravel.

Cod and halibut are the principal food fishes taken, hake, haddock, and cusk being taken in small numbers. The Rocky Bottom, a shoal ground of 20 to 25 fathom depths on the eastern part, was much resorted to by dory handliners in summer. The cod are most plentiful on the eastern part of the bank, though occasional good fares are taken toward the west. The best cod fishing on this bank is from May until September, when the schools gather to feed upon the lant, squid, crustaceans, and shellfish, then very abundant.

Halibut are found here all the year off the edges in 100 to 400 fathoms. Apparently these are feeding and breeding grounds for this species, and it is not unusual for a school to remain for weeks and even months in one locality, though some of these may be fish in migration northward.

The principal halibut grounds are along the southern and eastern borders of the bank—the Southwest Prong and the Southwest Cove (in about 44° N. lat. and between 58° 30' and 58° 55' W. long), the Middle Prong (44° 14' N. lat. and 58° W. long.), and the Eastern Slope (44° 28' to 45° 00' N. lat.)—in depths of 150 to 400 fathoms. These deep-water areas are rocky and support a very rich growth of gorgonians, corals, sea anemones, etc. The Eastern Slope has an abundance of bank clams in depths of 25 fathoms. These beds are good hand-line grounds for cod. The halibut, too, feeds to a considerable extent upon these red clams.

The Stone Fence off the eastern slope of Quereau is a very rocky piece of ground full of "trees" (corals) in 250 fathoms. This is a good halibut ground although it is almost impossible to haul the gear by hand and the use of the "gurdy" (a roller turned by a crank and fastened to the dory's bow for winding up the trawl) becomes necessary. Occasional fares of halibut are taken on and about the Rocky Bottom in 20 to 25 fathoms from July 1 to August 1.

The Gully. This is the deep waterway between Banquereau and Sable Island or Western Bank. It extends in an WNW. and an ESE. direction north of Sable Island, turning somewhat abruptly S. at its eastern end and continuing down between the eastern end of Western Bank and the Southwest Prong of Banquereau. The entire length is about 80 miles, the greatest width about 20 miles. Depths range from 68 to 145 fathoms over a bottom of rocks, gravel, sand, and mud. The rocky and gravelly portions form several ridges separated by areas of finer materials, except in the eastern section, where the intervals between are mostly covered by pebbles and sharp rocks. Ocean currents are generally westerly, of varying strength, much affected by the easterly winds.

The Gully is a very important halibut ground. The halibut are not found in great numbers all over the ground, perhaps the best of the fishing being on the rocky and gravelly ridges and slopes included between the meridians of 69° and 80° west longitude. This rocky bottom is rich in food, and the lant and herring are usually plentiful here in their season. In the spring the halibut seem to be especially numerous in the northern and northwestern parts of the bank, later, in June and July, moving farther out. Some, are found here in winter. While the cod is sometimes found in The Gully in 60 to 90 fathoms, it does not seem to be of regular occurrence; and apparently there are almost no haddock here, probably because of the depth of the water and the nature of the bottom.

Artimon Bank. Has an area of some 120 square miles with a bottom of gravel and rocks and depths of 38 to 50 fathoms. It is but little known because of the tendency of the fishermen to use the larger grounds close at hand. Cod are known to be present here, however. The bank lies N. of the eastern part of Quereau, separated from it by a narrow, deep-water channel.

Misaine Bank. Lies N. of the western two-thirds of Quereau, at one place very near, but in general the banks are separated by some 20 miles of deep water. Its greatest length is 80 miles and its greatest width 40 miles. Depths are from 40 to 60 fathoms over a bottom broken and rocky. It is not of much importance as a fishing ground, although a few halibut trips are landed from it in most years.

Canso Bank. A long, narrow extension of Misaine Bank, lying in an E, and W. direction; its length is 45 miles and its greatest width 13 miles, its area being about 425 square miles. Depths range from 30 to 65 fathoms over a bottom of sand, with spots of gravel and pebbles. It is not of much importance as a fishing ground, especially as judged by the use of it by the American fleet, though more fished by vessels from Nova Scotia; perhaps it is overshadowed by the presence of its larger neighbors, Western and Quereau Banks, with which grounds it forms virtually one piece of bottom, only narrow, deep-water channels separating them. These larger grounds are heavily fished both by American vessels and by those from Nova Scotia ports as well as by French and English otter trawlers.

The statistics given here and elsewhere in this report are taken from the published bulletins of the United States Bureau of Fisheries, and include only the landings of vessels of 5 tons net, or over, at the ports of Boston and Glouscester, Mass., and Portland, Me.

Table 5—Fishing grounds of the offshore North Atlantic, showing the principal species taken upon them.

Fishing ground	Cod	Haddock	Hake	Pollock	Cusk	Halibut	Herring	Mackerel	Lobsters	Miscellaneous
Browns Bank	x	x	x	x	x	x				[1] x
Seal Island Ground	x	x	x		x	x	[2] x	[3] x		
Roseway	x	x	x	x	x	x				
La Have Bank	x	x			x	x				
La Have Ridges; Little La Have	x		x			x				
Scandinavian Bank	x	x	x	x	x	x				
Western Bank	x	x		x		x				
Banquereau	x					x				
The Gully	x					x				
Artimon	x									
Missine	x									
Canso	x	x	x	x	x	x				

[1] Swordfish makes a considerable part of this.
[2] Food fish; very little taken by United States crafts.
[3] On shore soundings.

TABLES OF CATCH

Table 6—Distance from Boston or Gloucester, Mass., to the center of certain of the more important offshore banks

Bank	Miles	Bank	Miles
Georges	172	Emerald	375
Browns	220	Sable Island	470
Roseway	290	Quereau	555
La Have	315	Grand	928

Table 7—Distance from Portland, Me., to the center of certain of the more important offshore banks

Bank	Miles	Bank	Miles
Georges	180	Emerald	340
Browns	200	Sable Island	438
Roseway	250	Quereau	508
La Have	262	Grand	884

Table 8—Landings by fishing vessels at Boston and Gloucester, Mass., and Portland, Me., from inner or shore grounds, 1927

Species	Boston			Gloucester		
	Trips	Pounds	Value	Trips	Pounds	Value
Cod		398, 737	$14, 782		5, 060, 590	$246, 839
Haddock		2, 203, 170	70, 025		1, 630, 750	62, 441
Hake		193, 005	4, 254		80, 050	1, 564
Pollock		30, 963	741		3, 481, 835	70, 510
Cusk		60, 464	1, 898			
Halibut		11, 609	2, 472			
Mackerel		198, 445	20, 154		9, 958, 445	392, 166
Miscellaneous		2, 940, 109	118, 889		1, 700, 240	54, 508
Total	605	6, 036, 502	233, 215	3, 282	21, 911, 910	828, 028

Table 8—continued

Species	Portland			Total		
	Trips	Pounds	Value	Trips	Pounds	Value
Cod		1, 204, 112	$50, 091		6, 663, 439	$311, 712
Haddock		1, 101, 831	34, 528		4, 935, 751	166, 994
Hake		161, 941	3, 487		434, 996	9, 305
Pollock		286, 665	4, 361		3, 799, 463	75, 612
Cusk		155, 945	5, 043		216, 409	6, 941
Halibut		3, 643	769		15, 252	3, 241
Mackerel		196, 379	6, 246		10, 355, 269	418, 566
Miscellaneous		960, 238	22, 590		6, 600, 587	195, 987
Total	876	4, 072, 754	127, 115	4, 763	32, 021, 166	1, 188, 358

Note—The catch from these inner or shore grounds represents 46.87 per cent of the total values of the catch from all grounds at the 3 ports for the year 1927.

Table 9—Landings by fishing vessels at Boston and Gloucester, Mass.,
and Portland, Me., from the outer grounds of the Gulf of Maine, 1927

Species	Platts Bank			Cashes Bank			Jeffreys Ledge		
	Trips	Pounds	Value	Trips	Pounds	Value	Trips	Pounds	Value
Cod		187, 515	$8, 547		284, 204	$11, 190		1, 007, 016	$44, 340
Haddock		601, 021	30, 851		288, 318	11, 479		2, 260, 950	96, 198
Hake		210, 940	6, 296		110, 863	4, 488		550, 437	14, 617
Pollock		87, 480	1, 382		19, 235	392		459, 726	8, 195
Cusk		86, 542	3, 249		331, 914	10, 731		231, 565	7, 191
Halibut		2, 057	491		15, 760	2, 942		4, 647	905
Mackerel								243, 792	8, 486
Miscellaneous		76, 788	1, 396		11, 591	347		1, 623, 888	25, 762
Total	123	1, 252, 343	52, 212	63	1, 041, 885	41, 569	652	6, 382, 021	205, 694
Boston				8	256, 604	12, 828	99	1, 515, 386	67, 749
Portland	123	1, 252, 343	52, 212	55	785, 281	28, 743	553	4, 866, 635	137, 945

Species	Fippenies Bank			Tillies Bank		
	Trips	Pounds	Value	Trips	Pounds	Value
Cod		37, 555	$1, 751		500	$38
Haddock		129, 679	7, 086		6, 220	491
Hake		16, 154	564		2, 800	168
Pollock		11, 200	203		135	5
Cusk		14, 870	687		250	10
Halibut		2, 461	527			
Mackerel					138, 975	12, 185
Miscellaneous		2, 725	122		115	19
Total	24	214, 644	10, 940	10	148, 995	12, 916
Boston				10	148, 995	12, 916
Portland	24	214, 644	10, 940			

Table 9—continued

Species	Middle Bank [1]			Total		
	Trips	Pounds	Value	Trips	Pounds	Value
Cod		90, 910	$4, 583		1, 607, 700	$70, 449
Haddock		567, 290	27, 656		3, 833, 478	173, 761
Hake		99, 155	3, 580		990, 349	29, 713
Pollock		19, 930	597		597, 706	10, 774
Cusk		34, 220	1, 234		699, 361	23, 102
Halibut		1, 204	442		26, 129	5, 307
Mackerel		1, 001, 588	35, 719		1, 384, 355	55, 850
Miscellaneous		20, 965	1, 048		1, 736, 072	28, 694
Total	74	1, 835, 262	74, 319	946	10, 875, 150	397, 650
Boston	69	1, 616, 302	68, 972	186	3, 537, 287	162, 463
Gloucester	5	218, 960	5, 347	5	218, 960	5, 347
Portland				755	7, 118, 903	229, 840

[1] Known also as Stellwagen.

Note—In the totals for the year 1927 the catch for this group of grounds represents 9.39 per cent of all areas, 4.12 per cent of the poundage, and 4.23 per cent of the value at the 3 ports.

Table 10—Landings by fishing vessels at Boston and Gloucester, Mass.,

and Portland, Me., from the fishing grounds of the Georges Bank area, 1927

Species	Georges Bank			South Channel			Nantucket Shoals		
	Trips	Pounds	Value	Trips	Pounds	Value	Trips	Pounds	Value
Cod		24, 273, 869	$752, 145		12, 238, 525	$468, 133		868, 280	$29, 228
Haddock		8, 801, 380	229, 635		94, 978, 623	2, 509, 331		6, 246, 280	185, 462
Hake		87, 570	2, 262		3, 993, 676	107, 296		72, 755	1, 850
Pollock		984, 010	21, 746		1, 888, 632	56, 193		50, 885	1, 002
Cusk		295, 765	5, 459		459, 515	14, 621		1, 150	40
Halibut		1, 066, 760	204, 361		268, 999	58, 593		14, 889	2, 092
Mackerel		934, 420	96, 114		4, 078, 460	176, 777		168, 470	5, 555
Miscellaneous		1, 709, 012	354, 079		3, 782, 263	216, 414		1, 054, 708	71, 825
Total	963	38, 152, 786	1, 665, 801	2, 036	121, 688, 693	3, 607, 358	216	8, 477, 417	297, 054
Boston	786	31, 004, 619	1, 477, 364	1, 918	112, 095, 440	3, 470, 255	189	7, 606, 212	276, 440
Gloucester	164	6, 855, 508	162, 628	102	6, 625, 205	91, 065	24	640, 560	16, 996
Portland	13	292, 659	25, 809	16	2, 968, 048	46, 038	3	230, 645	3, 618

Species	Off Cape Cod			Total		
	Trips	Pounds	Value	Trips	Pounds	Value
Cod		107, 640	$3, 952		37, 488, 314	$1, 253, 458
Haddock		1, 866, 970	63, 252		111, 893, 253	2, 987, 680
Hake		40, 820	1, 645		4, 194, 821	113, 053
Pollock		12, 675	349		2, 936, 202	79, 290
Cusk		11, 150	339		767, 580	20, 459
Halibut		1, 364	274		1, 352, 012	265, 320
Mackerel		4, 471, 641	237, 637		9, 652, 991	516, 083
Miscellaneous		205, 523	11, 532		6, 751, 506	653, 850
Total	284	6, 717, 783	318, 980	3, 499	175, 036, 679	5, 889, 193
Boston	284	6, 717, 783	318, 980	3, 177	157, 424, 054	5, 543, 039
Gloucester				290	14, 121, 273	270, 689
Portland				32	3, 491, 352	75, 465

Note—In the totals showing value, poundage, and number of fares from all grounds, as taken out at Boston, Gloucester, and Portland for the year 1927, the catch from the Georges Bank area represents 34.43 per cent of the fares, 62.62 per cent of the value and 66.34 per cent of the poundage.

Table 11—Landings by the otter-trawl fleet at Boston and Gloucester, Mass., and Portland, Me., from the fishing grounds of the Georges Bank area, 1927

Species	Georges Bank			South Channel			Nantucket Shoals		
	Trips	Pounds	Value	Trips	Pounds	Value	Trips	Pounds	Value
Cod	....	178, 987	$6, 435	....	3, 709, 688	$144, 123	....	88, 230	$3, 275
Haddock	....	1, 380, 685	42, 933	....	63, 593, 777	1, 651, 498	....	3, 908, 690	119, 757
Hake	....	1, 895	49	....	947, 110	27, 543	....	45, 225	1, 045
Pollock	....	15, 840	727	....	1, 077, 545	38, 987	....	14, 100	443
Cusk	....	....	....	....	11, 440	440	....	175	6
Halibut	....	2, 405	712	....	94, 796	23, 542	....	1, 556	380
Miscellaneous	....	34, 720	2, 612	....	2, 000, 773	127, 196	....	86, 982	5, 142
Total	17	1, 584, 532	53, 468	736	71, 435, 129	2, 013, 329	39	4, 144, 958	130, 048

Species	Off Cape Cod			Total		
	Trips	Pounds	Value	Trips	Pounds	Value
Cod	....	6, 000	$240	....	3, 982, 905	$154, 073
Haddock	....	111, 700	6, 612	....	68, 964, 852	1, 820, 800
Hake	....	500	40	....	994, 730	28, 677
Pollock	....	240	17	....	1, 107, 725	40, 174
Cusk	....	....	....	....	11, 615	446
Halibut	....	10	2	....	98, 767	24, 636
Miscellaneous	....	21, 570	1, 436	....	2, 144, 045	136, 386
Total	1	140, 020	8, 347	793	77, 304, 639	2, 205, 192

Note—In the year's totals from all grounds at these ports the catch from this area by otter trawls represents 29.30 per cent of the poundage, 23.42 per cent of the value, and 7.80 per cent of the number of fares. In the totals for this area the otter trawl accounts for 44.16 per cent of the poundage, 37.44 per cent of the value, and 22.66 per cent of fares. Apparently but 1 other otter trawl was reported at these ports for the year, and that was from the Western Bank and totaled 178,987 pounds of haddock, valued at $2,410.

Table 12—Landings by fishing vessels at Boston and Gloucester, Mass., and Portland, Me., from the offshore grounds adjacent to the Gulf of Maine, 1927

Species	Browns Bank			Seal Island Ground			La Have Bank		
	Trips	Pounds	Value	Trips	Pounds	Value	Trips	Pounds	Value
Cod	....	6, 334, 143	$203, 047	....	52, 265	$2, 836	....	4, 148, 851	$133, 889
Haddock	....	4, 168, 035	120, 458	....	35, 440	1, 511	....	2, 185, 471	57, 060
Hake	....	50, 380	1, 203	....	1, 200	12	....	104, 055	1, 634
Pollock	....	175, 335	3, 443	....	875	14	....	85, 635	1, 775
Cusk	....	684, 670	13, 462	....	7, 400	204	....	243, 075	5, 356
Halibut	....	204, 237	40, 742	....	130	39	....	216, 015	38, 968
Miscellaneous	....	473, 421	79, 915	....	....	....	....	72, 909	8, 272
Total	226	12, 090, 221	462, 270	2	97, 310	4, 616	119	7, 056, 011	246, 963
Boston	183	9, 673, 691	412, 118	2	97, 310	4, 616	81	3, 979, 418	192, 872
Gloucester	37	2, 091, 964	34, 778	....	....	....	36	3, 015, 737	50, 415
Portland	6	324, 566	15, 374	....	....	....	2	60, 856	3, 676

Table 12—continued

Species	⸱e Shore			Sable Island area					
				Western Bank			The Gully		
	Trips	Pounds	Value	Trips	Pounds	Value	Trips	Pounds	Value
Cod	....	308, 770	$14, 187	....	6, 032, 690	$131, 798	....	3, 981	$129
Haddock	....	122, 885	4, 679	....	1, 383, 400	18, 876	....	320	6
Hake	....	6, 370	235	....	43, 385	786	....	2, 300	92
Pollock	....	9, 745	206	....	54, 205	648	....	360	14
Cusk	....	10, 545	149	....	26, 725	402	....	....	....
Halibut	....	1, 142	338	....	142, 898	23, 024	....	61, 965	12, 564
Mackerel	....	197, 400	4, 381	....	....	....	....	....	....
Miscellaneous	....	254, 577	58, 324	....	5, 048	290	....	....	....
Total	48	911, 434	82, 499	95	7, 688, 351	175, 824	2	68, 926	12, 805
Boston	34	732, 492	65, 309	49	1, 083, 260	51, 053	1	42, 767	7, 665
Gloucester	....	....	....	....	....	111, 896	....	....	....
Portland	14	178, 942	17.	....	....	12, 875	1	26, 156	5, 140

Species	Sable Island area			Total		
	Quereau Bank					
	Trips	Pounds	Value	Trips	Pounds	Value
Cod	....	384, 706	$12, 751	....	17, 265, 406	$498, 637
Haddock	....	34, 350	675	....	7, 929, 901	203, 274
Hake	....	19, 060	304	....	226, 750	4, 266
Pollock	....	1, 640	31	....	327, 795	6, 131
Cusk	....	59, 892	1, 059	....	1, 032, 307	20, 632
Halibut	....	909, 838	149, 072	....	1, 536, 225	264, 747
Mackerel	....	....	....	....	197, 400	4, 381
Miscellaneous	....	12, 307	781	....	818, 202	147, 582
Total	53	1, 421, 793	164, 673	555	29, 334, 046	1, 149, 650
Boston	33	891, 194	132, 842	376	16, 500, 132	866, 475
Gloucester	24	419, 653	14, 164	146	11, 408, 259	211, 253
Portland	6	110, 946	17, 667	33	1, 425, 655	71, 922

Note—The totals for the group of grounds shown here represent 11.12 per cent of the poundage, 12.22 per cent of the value, and 5.46 per cent of the number of fares from all grounds at these 3 ports for 1927. For the Sable Island area, 9,179,070 pounds, valued at $353,302; 160 fares make 2.48, 3.75, and 1.57 per cent, respectively.

Table 13—Landings by fishing vessels at Boston and Gloucester, Mass., and Portland, Me., from all grounds, 1927

Species	Boston			Gloucester		
	Trips	Pounds	Value	Trips	Pounds	Value
Cod		40,309,673	$1,458,930		20,249,074	$574,540
Haddock		109,860,353	3,149,069		11,312,771	187,989
Hake		4,779,441	131,285		228,280	3,283
Pollock		3,201,525	86,112		3,645,570	72,258
Cusk		1,680,124	44,905		356,232	4,906
Halibut		4,320,036	764,079		42,882	3,492
Mackerel		20,444,080	863,185		10,554,395	416,970
Miscellaneous [1]		10,345,557	873,977		6,163,336	230,497
Total	4,684	194,940,789	7,371,542	3,772	52,552,540	1,493,935

[1] Under this heading various species are listed, mostly in small amounts. The most important are flounders, 8,359,131 pounds, valued at $419,744; herring, 7,145,436 pounds, valued at $200,736; and swordfish, 2,245,493 pounds, valued at $513,582.

Table 13—continued

Species	Portland			Total		
	Trips	Pounds	Value	Trips	Pounds	Value
Cod		2,795,982	$113,033		63,354,729	$2,146,503
Haddock		7,419,559	194,655		128,592,683	3,531,713
Hake		824,905	21,977		5,832,626	156,545
Pollock		815,286	13,479		7,662,361	171,849
Cusk		690,861	21,563		2,727,217	71,374
Halibut		416,365	72,374		4,779,283	839,945
Mackerel		531,416	15,392		31,529,891	1,295,547
Miscellaneous [1]		2,831,890	86,561		19,340,783	1,191,035
Total	1,706	16,356,244	539,034	10,162	263,849,573	9,404,511

[1] Under this heading various species are listed, mostly in small amounts. The most important are flounders, 8,359,131 pounds, valued at $419,744; herring, 7,145,436 pounds, valued at $200,736; and swordfish, 2,245,493 pounds, valued at $513,582.

Table 14—Landings by fishing vessels from the various fishing grounds at Boston and Gloucester, Mass., and Portland, Me., 1927

Fishing ground	Trips	Pounds	Value	Fishing ground	Trips	Pounds	Value
Labrador	2	101,268	$10,608	Georges Bank	963	38,152,786	$1,665,801
Belle Isle	1	7,500	246	Off Highland	55	812,797	79,479
Off Newfoundland	17	4,533,284	177,051	Off Chatham	229	5,904,986	239,503
Grand Bank	40	953,717	134,134	South Channel	2,036	121,688,693	3,607,358
Green Bank	7	173,105	25,059	Nantucket Shoals	216	8,477,417	297,054
St. Peters Bank	22	720,177	113,884	Cashes Bank	63	1,041,885	41,569
St. Anns Bank	1	32,958	4,817	Fippenies Bank	24	214,644	10,940
St. Lawrence	2	63,261	8,810	New Ledge	123	1,252,343	52,212
Quereau Bank	63	1,421,793	164,673	Jeffreys Ledge	652	6,382,021	205,694
The Gully	2	68,926	12,805	Tillies Bank	10	148,995	12,916
Western Bank	95	7,688,351	175,824	Middle Bank	74	1,835,262	74,319
La Have Bank	119	7,056,011	246,963	Shore, general	4,763	32,021,166	1,188,358
Cape Shore	48	911,434	82,499	South	306	9,962,886	301,547
Roseway	2	34,358	3,504				
Browns Bank	226	12,090,221	462,270	Total	10,162	263,849,573	9,404,511
Seal Island Ground	2	97,310	4,616				

Table 15—Landings by fishing vessels from all grounds at Boston and Gloucester, Mass., and Portland, Me., 1916 to 1927

Year	Boston			Gloucester		
	Trips	Pounds	Value	Trips	Pounds	Value
1916	3,089	96,331,038	$3,702,365	2,864	66,680,548	$2,159,894
1917	2,962	98,650,139	5,166,440	3,074	58,134,944	2,451,484
1918	2,830	109,476,041	6,587,754	3,414	74,175,499	3,062,605
1919	2,754	103,391,370	4,713,350	2,965	71,370,957	2,145,592
1920	3,342	118,558,902	6,136,569	2,381	46,740,296	1,460,336
1921	3,078	104,368,629	4,190,135	2,073	33,016,166	920,250
1922	2,893	106,190,403	4,020,105	1,653	37,751,223	813,353
1923	3,368	124,215,034	5,433,731	1,579	35,029,848	910,739
1924	3,735	130,966,256	5,401,590	2,157	35,845,920	1,041,476
1925	4,404	149,038,498	6,104,278	2,491	49,471,943	1,390,580
1926	4,569	167,317,826	7,002,602	2,665	54,900,824	1,479,312
1927	4,684	194,940,789	7,371,542	3,772	52,552,540	1,493,935

Table 15—continued

Year	Portland			Total		
	Trips	Pounds	Value	Trips	Pounds	Value
1916	2,992	20,812,839	$521,647	8,945	185,824,425	$6,383,906
1917	3,248	18,645,503	743,408	9,284	175,430,586	8,361,332
1918	2,506	21,849,613	881,189	8,750	205,501,153	10,531,548
1919	2,550	21,718,943	689,441	8,269	196,481,270	7,548,383
1920	1,883	12,961,503	630,108	7,606	178,280,701	8,227,013
1921	2,055	13,480,311	612,244	7,206	150,865,106	5,722,620
1922	1,803	15,933,765	632,474	6,349	159,875,391	5,465,932
1923	1,588	15,696,587	706,684	6,535	174,941,469	7,051,154
1924	1,583	16,136,018	549,886	7,475	182,948,194	6,992,952
1925	1,509	18,358,824	620,712	8,404	216,869,265	8,115,570
1926	1,461	16,207,573	575,760	8,695	238,426,223	9,057,674
1927	1,706	16,356,244	539,034	10,182	263,849,573	9,404,511

MAPS

Coastal Banks and Inshore Grounds of the Gulf of Maine
Bay of Fundy

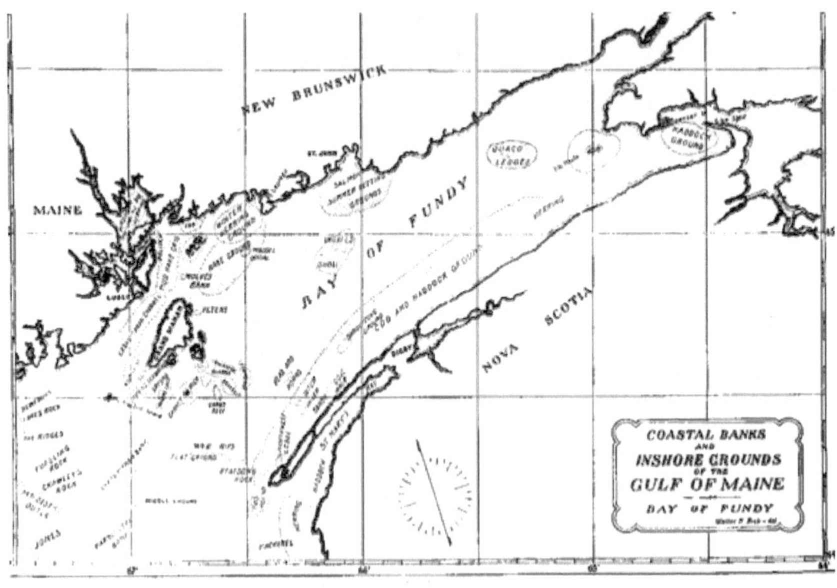

Coastal Banks and Inshore Grounds of the Gulf of Maine
Monhegan to Petit Manan

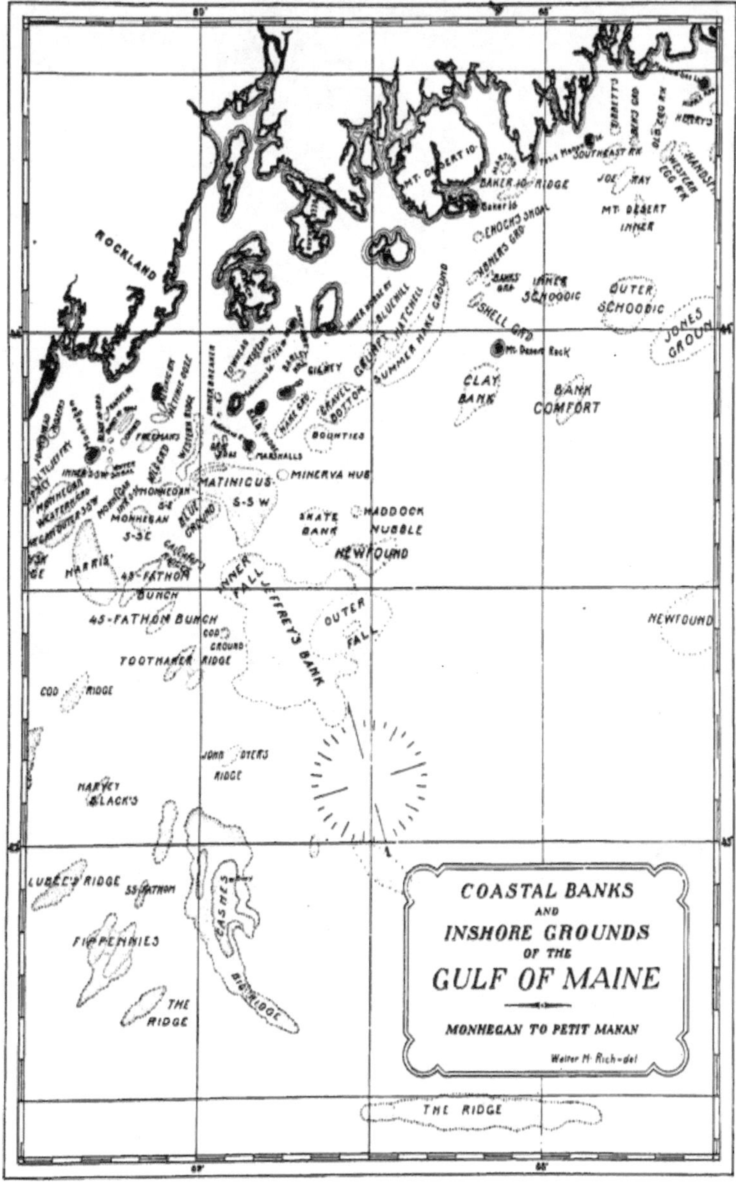

Coastal Banks and Inshore Grounds of the Gulf of Maine
Monhegan to Cape Cod

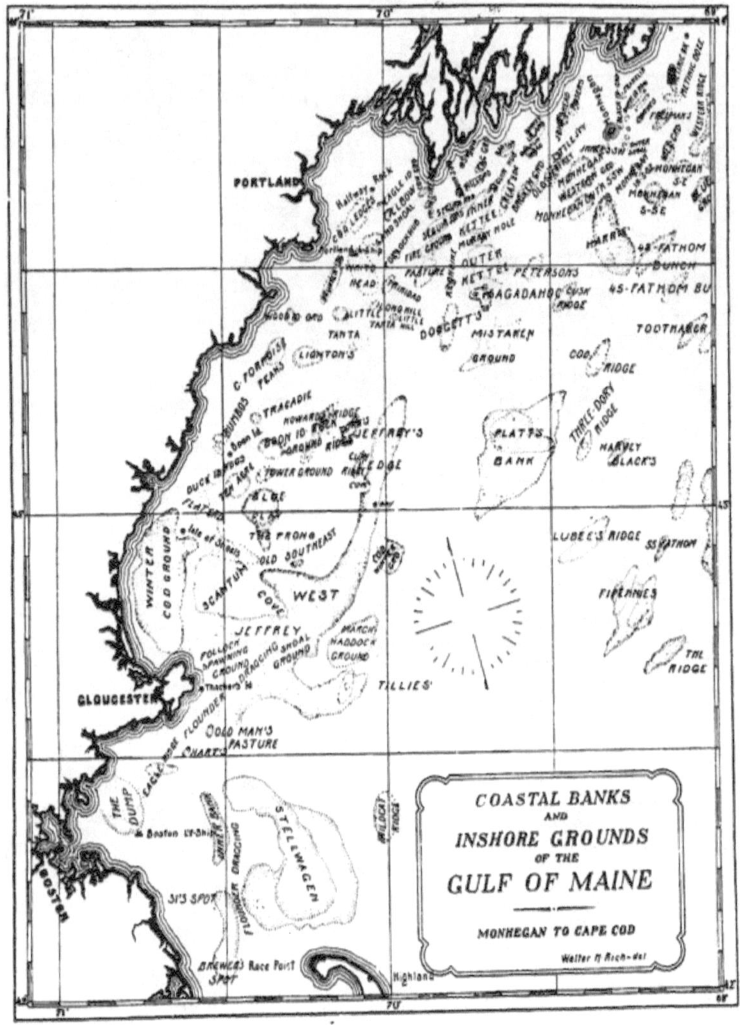

Coastal Banks and Inshore Grounds of the Gulf of Maine
Petit Manan to Seal Island

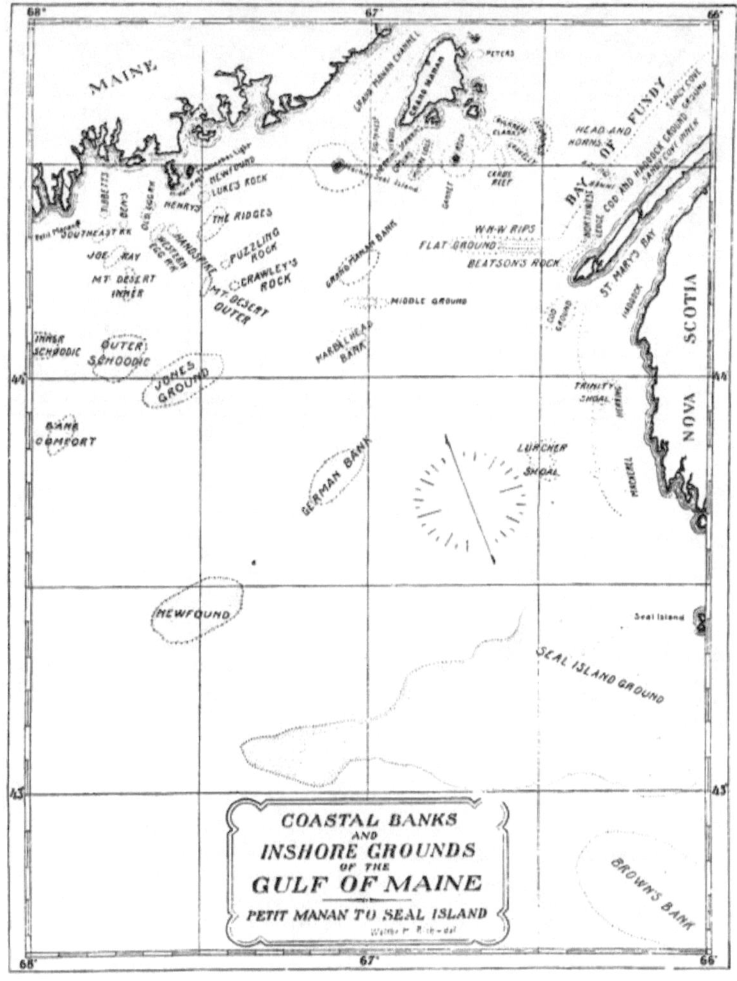

Fishing Grounds of the Gulf of Maine
The Georges Area

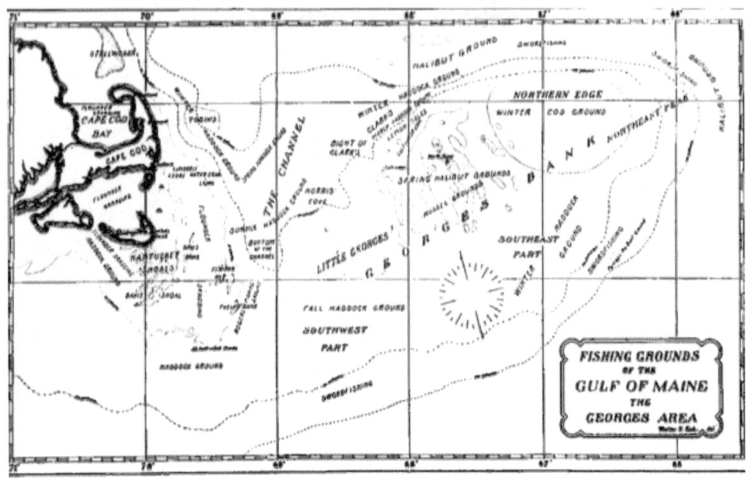

FOOTNOTES

Footnote 2: U.S. Bureau of Fisheries Statistical Bulletin No. 703

Footnote 3: U.S. Bureau of Fisheries Document No. 1034

Footnote 4: "All that parte, purport and porcion of the Mayne Land of New England, we doe name, ordeyne and appoynt shall forever hereafter bee called and named The Province and Countie of Mayne."

Footnote 5: *Edinburgh Encyclopedia*, Philadelphia edition, by Thomas Parker, Vol. XVIII, p. 263.

Footnote 6: William Strachey (1609), speaking particularly of Casco Bay, but the words equally applicable to almost any stretch of the Maine coast, says "A very great bay in which there lyeth soe many islands and soe thick and neere together, that can hardly be discerned the number, yet may any ship pause betwixt, the greatest part of them having seldom lesse water than eight or ten fathoms about them" —*History of Travalle into Virginia Britannica.*

Footnote 7: This, the most striking cape of the Atlantic coast line, made a very prominent landmark for all the early ocean voyagers approaching it, and all were greatly impressed by it, whether they came from the south and fought their way through its shoals to eastward, or, coming from the north, found themselves caught in the deep pocket which it makes with Cape Cod Bay.

The Spaniard Gomez (1525) gave it the name "Cabo de do Aricifes" cape of the reefs, referring to the dangerous shoals to the eastward. The Frenchmen Champlain and Du Monts named it "Cape Blanc", and the Dutch pilots, also noting its sandy cliffs, called it Witte Hoeck. The English mariners at first accepted his last name of White Cape, but the English Captain Anthony Gosnold, the first to make a direct passage to the waters of the Gulf of Maine from Europe, although at first he called it "Shoal Hope", soon changed this, because of the success of his fishing, to "Cape Cod", which title, commonplace though it be, has been the name to endure despite Prince Charles's attempt to change it to Cape James in honor of his father.

Footnote 8: Cape Sable, at the southern end of Nova Scotia, has held this title from very old times. It is so indicated on a Portuguese map of the middle of the sixteenth century.

Footnote 9: It (Fundy) was not clearly indicated by Verrazano (1524) nor in the report of Gomez (1525), who probably saw something of its entrance but fog or other unfavorable circumstances may have prevented him from observing it more accurately, but we find in the first old Spanish maps, in the latitude where it ought to be, names like these:

Rio hondo or 'fondo' (a deep river) or Bahia Hondo (a deep bay), or Golfo (a gulf) once, also 'La Bahia de la ensenada', the bay of the deep inlet.

Doctor Kohl, here quoted further says "On the maps of the seventeenth and early part of the eighteenth century, especially, it is written Bay of Funda. I believe that this name grew out from and is a revival of, the old Spanish name 'Bahia fondo'".

Footnote 10: It is gratifying to announce that the winter of 1925-26 saw a large run of herring on this ground, where for a number of years past there has been virtually no fishing for this species.

Footnote 11: "According to Porter C. Bliss, a thorough student of the Indian dialects, Acadie is a pure Micmac word meaning place. In Nova Scotia and Maine it is used by the Indians in composition with other words, as in Pestum-Acadie; and in Etchemin, Pascatum-Acadie, now Passamaquoddy, meaning 'the place of the pollocks'" (Doctor Kohl, *Dis. of Maine*, p. 234)

"This derivation is doubtful. The Micmac word Quoddy, Kady, or Cadie means simply a place or region and is properly used in conjunction with some other noun; as, for example, Pestum-oquoddy (Passamaquoddy), the place of pollocks." (Dawson and Hand, in *Canadian Antiquarian and Numismatic Journal*)

"La Cadie, or Arcadie: The word is said to be derived from the Indian Aquoddiaukie, or Aquoddie, supposed to mean the fish called a pollock. The Bay of Passamaquoddy, 'great pollock water,' if we may accept the same authority, derives its name from the same origin." (Potter, in *Historical Magazine*, I, 84)

Footnote 12: Again, Captain Smith (1614): "At the Ile of Manahigan, in 43 1/2 of Northerly latitude . . . The remarkablest isle, and mountains for landmarks, a round high isle, with little Monas by its side, betwixt which is a small harbor, where our ships can lie at anchor." [Transcriber's note: "Ile" is as spelled in the footnote, despite the other spellings of it in the footnote as "isle."]

Footnote 13: There has been some speculation as to the origin of the somewhat unusual name of this bank. The writer would note that there was an Edward Tillie in the Company of Captain John Smith when he explored this region in 1614 and a Tilly (perhaps the same person) who operated a fishing station at Cape Ann during the years 1624 and 1625.

Footnote 14: Capt. John Smith wrote of this region: "Toward the South and Southwest of this Cape [Cape Cod] is found a long and dangerous shoal of sands and rocks. But so far as I incircled it, I found thirtie fadom water aboard the shore, and a strong current; which makes mee thinke there is a Channell about the shoales; where is the best and greatest fish to be had, Winter and Summer in all that Countree. But the Savages say there is no Channell; but that the shoales begin from the main at Pawmet, to the Ile of Nausit; and so extends beyond their knowledge into the sea." That the captain's reputation for far-visioned wisdom may not be held too lightly, let these figures speak, taken as they are from the bureau's records of the landings at the three ports of Boston, Gloucester. and Portland for the year 1927, when the fares from his "Channell" numbered 2,036, with a poundage of 121,688,693 and a value of $3,607,358.

Footnote 15: 'The earliest record of this name (Saint Georges Shoal) that the writer has found appears upon a map discovered in the library of Simancas, in Spain, where a chart said to have been made by a surveyor sent out to Virginia by James I of England, in 1610, was found in 1885 or 1888, after having long before disappeared from England. This chart is thought to embody, besides the work of Champlain and other foreigners, the information contained in the English charts of White, Gosnold, Pring, and probably of Waymouth's Perfect Geographical Map. It is thought to have been drawn by Robert Tyndall or Captain Powell. *Genesis of the United States*. Alexander Brown.

Footnote 16: "Pedro Reinel, a Portuguese pilot of much fame" (Herrera) made a map in 1505 showing Sable Island, feared and dreaded by all fishermen even in those days, where he called it "Santa Cruz." Jacamo Gastaldi, an Italian cartographer, in 1548 shows it "Isolla de Arena." Sir Humphrey Gilbert or his historian, says that the Portuguese had made an interesting settlement here for shipwrecked mariners. This, "Upon intelligence we had of a Portugal who was himself present when the Portugals, above thirty years past [thus before 1551] did put upon the island neat and swine to breed, which were since exceedingly multiplied."

INDEX TO GROUNDS

Bumbo, Outer and Inner
Burnt Island Inner Ridge
Burnt Island Outer Ridge
Bull Ground
Campobello
Canso
Cape Porpoise Peaks
Cards Reef
Cashes Bank
Cashes Ridge, East
Cashes NW Ridge
Cashes Big Ridge
Channel
Clarks Ground
Clay Bank
Clay Ridge
Coast of Nova Scotia
Cod Ledges
Cod Ridge
Cove (S.E. Jeffreys)
Cove (W. Jeffreys)
Cow Ground
Crab Bank
Crie Ridges
Cusk Ridge
Davis Bank
Deckers Shoal
Doggetts Ridge
Drunken Ledge (Drunkers)
Duck Island Ridges
Dump, The
Eagle Island Ground
Eagle Ridge
Eastern Shoal Water, Cape Ann
East Side Cape Cod
Egg Rock Broken Ground
Elbow, The
Enochs Shoal
Fifty-five Fathom
Fippenies

Fire Ground

Fishing Rip

Flat Ground

Flat Ledge

Forty-five Fathom

Franklin Ground

Freemans Ground

Gannet Rock

Garden, The

Georges Bank

German Bank

Gilkey Ground

Grand Manan

Grand Manan Bank

Gravel Bottom

Gravelley

Great Ledge

Great Rip

Green Ground

Green Island Ridge

Grumpy

Gully, The

Haddock Nubble

Hake Ground

Handspike Ground

Harris Ground

Harts Ground

Harvey Blacks Ridge

Hatchell Ground

Head and Horns

Henry Gallants Ridge

Henry Marshalls

Henrys Rock

Hill Ground

Howard Nunans Ridge

Hue and Cry

Ingalls Shoal

Inner Bank

Inner and Outer Boutens

Inner Breaker

Inner and Outer Bumbo
Inner Fall
Inner Grounds
Inner Horse Reef
Inner Kettle
Inner Sandy Cove
Inner Schoodic Ridge
Ipswich Bay
Isle au Haute (Ca)
Jeffreys Bank
Jeffreys Ledge
Jerry Yorks Ridge
Joe Ray Ground
John Dyers Ridge
Johns Head Ground
Jones Ground
Kettle Bottom, Outer
Kettle Bottom, Inner
Klondike
Laisdells Ground
Lambo
La Have
La Have Ridges
Lightons
Little Hill Ground
Little Georges
Little Jeffrey
Little La Have
Long Hill Ground
Lukes Rock
Lurcher Shoal
Machias Seal Island
Madisons Spot
Marblehead Bank
Martins Ground
Massachusetts Bay
Matinic Bank
Matinic Ooze
Matinicus SSW
Maurice Lubees Ridge

McIntire Reef
Middle Bank
Middle Ground
Middle Ridge
Middle Shoal
Minerva Hub
Misaine Bank
Mistaken Ground
Monhegan Inner SSE
Monhegan Outer SSE
Monhegan Southeast
Monhegan Inner SSW
Monhegan Outer SSW
Monhegan Western Ground
Morris Ledge
Mosers Ledge
Mount Desert Inner Ridge
Mount Desert Outer Ridge
Mud Hake Grounds
Murray Hole
Murre Hub
Mussel Shoal
Nantucket Shoals
Newfound Ground (Fundy)
Newfound Ground (MDI)
New Ledge
New Meadows Channel
Nipper Ground
North Shore of Nova Scotia
Northwest Ledge
Old Egg Rock
Old Jeffrey
Old Mans Pasture
Old Orchard Ground
Old Ripper
Old Southeast
Ornes Ground
Otter Island Reef
Outer Bumbo
Outer Boutens

Outer Crab Ledge
Outer Ground
Outer Horse Reef
Outer Kettle
Outer Schoodic Ridge
Outer Shoal
Passamaquoddy Bay
Pasture
Peters Bank
Petersons Ground
Phelps Bank
Pigeon Ground
Platts Bank
Pollock Hub
Pollock Rip
Potato Patch
Prairie
Quaco Ledges
Quereau
Ridge, The Big
Ridge, East Cashes
Ridge, North Georges
Ridge, Northwest Cashes
Ridge, South Fippenies
Ridge, Three-dory
Ripplings
Rock Cod Ledge
Rose and Crown
Roseway
Saddleback Reef
Sagadahoc
Salmon Netting Ground
Sand Shoal
Sandy Cove
Scandinavian Bank
Scantum
Seal Island Ground
Seguin Ground
Seguin Hub
Seguin Ridge

Seguin SSW
Shoal Ground
Shell Ground
Si's Spot
Skate Bank
Snipper Shin
Soundings
Southeast
Southeast Ground
Southeast Jeffreys
Southeast Ledge
Southeast Rip
Southeast Rock
Southern Head Reef
South Shoal
Southwest Ground
Southwest Rock
Southwest Ledges
Spencer Island
Steamboat Ground
Stellwagen Bank
Stone Fence
Summer Hake Ground
Tag Ground
Tanta
Temple Ledge
Ten Acre
Three-dory Ridge
Tibbett's Ledge
Tillies Bank
Tobins Bank
Toothaker Ridge
Tower Ground
Towhead Ground
Tracadie
Trinidad
Trinity Shoal
Wells Bay
Western Bank
Western Egg Rock

Western Point Ridge
Western Reef
Western Ridge
White Head Grounds
White Island Ground
Wildcat Ridge
WNW Rips
Wolves
Wolves Bank
Wood Island Ground
Winker Ground

Geographic list of Gulf of Maine Fishing Grounds

BAY OF FUNDY AREA
Description of Fundy Area
North Shore and Nova Scotia coast
Lurcher Shoal
Trinity Shoal
Northwest Ledges
West-Northwest Rips & the Flat Ground
Boars Head Ground
Outer Ground Head and Horns
Sandy Cove Grounds
Inner Sandy Cove Grounds
Spencer Island Grounds
Isle au Haute Ground
Quaco Ledges
Salmon Netting Ground
Ingalls Shoal
Mussel Shoal Ground The Wolves
The Wolves Bank
Campobello
Passamaquoddy Bay
Mud Hake Ground
Beaver Harbor
Grand Manan
Clarks Bank
Southern Head Reef
Gravelly
Soundings

Bulkhead, Ripplings
Cards Reef
Gannet Rock
Southeast Ground
Machias Seal Island

INNER GULF OF MAINE AREA
Lukes Rock
Newfound Ground
Henrys Rock
Handspike Ground
Western Egg Rock
Old Egg Rock
Middle Ridge
Broken Ground
Tibbetts Ledge
Bens Ground
Southeast Rock
Broken Ridges.
Black Ledges Ground
Bakers Island Ridge
Martins Ground; Hillards Reef
Egg Rock Broken Ground
Inner Schoodic Ridge
Outer Schoodic Ridge
Mount Desert Inner Ridge
Mount Desert Outer Ridge
Flat Ground
Enochs Shoal
Banks Ground
Shell Ground
Abner Ground
Grumpy
Hatchell Ground
Blue Hill Ground
Hake Ground (Inner and Outer) Horse Reef
Southwest Ground
Barley Hill Ground
Gilkey Ground
Rock Cod Ledge

Southeast Gravel Bottom
Laisdells Ground
Saddleback Reef
Otter Island Reef
Old Ripper
Crie Ridges
Bald Ridges
Henry Marshalls Ground
The Bounties
Summer Hake Ground
Minerva Hub
Haddock Nubble
Skate Bank
Matinicus Sou'Sou'West
Inner Breaker
Towhead Grounds Western or Green Island Ridge & Pigeon Ground
Matinic Bank
Matinic Ooze
Freemans Ground
Middle Shoal, Allens Shoal, Black Island Ground
Franklin Ground
White Head Grounds
Burnt Island, Inner Ground
Burnt Island, Outer Ground
Ornes Ground
Outer Shoal
Monhegan Inner Sou'Southeast
Monhegan Outer
Sou'Southeast Blue Ground
Monhegan Southeast Ground
Hill Ground
Monhegan Inner Sou'Sou'West
Old Jeffrey
Little Jeffrey
Monhegan Western Ground
Broken Ground
Great Ledge
Barnum Head Ground
Peterson's Ground
Cusk Ridge

Potato Patch
The Apron
Henry Gallants Ridge
Middle Ground; Mosers
Johns Head Ground
White Island Ground
Steamboat Ground
Inner and Outer Boutens
Hill Ground
Seguin Sou' Sou'West
Seguin Ridge
Seguin Ground
McIntire Reef
Seguin Hub
Cow Ground
Murre Hub
Mistaken Ground
Tag Ground
Kettle Bottom, Outer
Murray Hole
Inner Kettle
Bantam
White Head Ground
Green Ground
Lambo
The Bull Ground
The Garden
Sand Shoal
The Elbow
Old Orchard; Wood Island Ground
Drunken Ledge

OUTER GULF OF MAINE AREA
Grand Manan Bank
Middle Ground
Marblehead Bank
Newfound
Jones Ground
Bank Comfort
Clay Bank

Newfound
Jeffreys Bank
Inner Fall
Toothaker Ridge
Cashes Bank
Ridge east of Cashes
Ridge northwest of Cashes
Big Ridge
Ridge north of Georges
John Dyers Ridge
Fifty-five Fathom Bunch
Fippenies Bank
Ridge south of Fippenie
Maurice Luhees Ground
Harvey Blacks Ridge
Cod Ridge
Three-Dory Ridge
Platts Bank
Jeffreys Ledge
Cove of Jeffreys
Clay Ridge
Jerry Yorks Ridge
Howard Howard Nunans Ridge
Southeast Jeffreys
Southeast Cove
Eastern Shoal Water of Cape Ann
Tillies Bank
Stellwagen or Middle Bank
Wild Cat Ridge

GEORGES BANK AREA
East Side of Cape Cod
Tobins Bank
Morris Ledge
Outer Crab Ledge
Nantucket Shoals
South Shoal
Pollock Rip Grounds
Rose & Crown
Nantucket Shoals—Madisons Spot

Nantucket Shoals—Great Rip
Nantucket Shoals—Davis Bank; Crab Bank
Nantucket Shoals—Fishing Rip
Nantucket Shoals—Southeast Rip
Phelps Bank
The Channel
Sankaty Head
Georges Bank

OFFSHORE BANKS
Browns Bank
Seal Island Ground
Roseway Bank
La Have Bank
Little La Have & the La Have Ridges
Scandinavian Bank
Western Bank
Banquereau
Stone Fence
The Gully
Artimon Bank
Misaine Bank
Canso Bank